A Ranchwife's Slant

Cowboys, Kids, & Ranchlife

A Ranchwife's Slant

Cowboys, Kids, & Ranchlife

By Amy Kirk

SPINNING SEVENS
PRESS

ISBN 978-0-9845850-6-9

Designed by Chris Legg
Cover photograph by Amy Kirk

Dedication

This book is dedicated to all of my column readers who have loyally taken time out of their day every week to read my column. Through my good columns and my bad columns, they stuck with me and, amazingly, continue to anticipate what I'll write about next. Without them, I could never have realized my dream of becoming a humor columnist about ranch life or publishing this book. I write with the intention of being the best part of each of my readers' day.

Contents

Part II: Kids

Part III: Ranch Life

Foreword

Amy Kirk is, in my opinion, the perfect ranch wife. Not only does she live an authentic ranch life, but she can write about it with wit and truth.

On my ranch on the prairie east of South Dakota's Black Hills, I began reading my manuscript copy of her book on a lovely October afternoon. Unknown to me, Amy was attending a conference of Women in Agriculture in Keystone, only a few miles away among the rocks and trees of the Hills. I'm sure we were both reluctant to be inside because the fall weather was perfect, the air clear, the grass and trees bright with autumn colors.

As Amy attended conference sessions and I read her words, the snow began to fall and the winds began to blow. Before it was over, we had each experienced the worst October snowstorm in South Dakota history. Because the power was off for several days, neither of us had any idea how severe the storm was. We adjusted to our situations, enjoying candlelight and quiet talk with out the lights and noise we've grown accustomed to in modern life.

Early the next week, Amy posted photographs of the ranch and farm women shoveling themselves out of the lodge parking lot as South Dakota residents were beginning to learn that the storm had killed thousands of head of livestock in the country we both write about, the western part of the state.

On her web site, amykirk.com, she later wrote "I have not been able to stop thinking about the number of cattle and other livestock that did not survive and the severity of damage in other areas due to the storm. It's left me with a sickening feeling for other livestock owners. Please pray for them as they try to recover from loss of livestock and the essence of their livelihood."

All across this and other western states, prayers will rise from the grasslands as ranchers and farmers survey these devastating losses. Some will say, "It coulda been worse." Agricultural sources say some ranchers have lost perhaps 50% of their herds. For years, those hardest hit will struggle to surmount this economic tragedy. For some, this single storm may mean the end of a business that is always run on a shoestring.

Since I spent part of the storm days reading Amy's book, and since I share her grief for the ranchers who have lost so much, I feel we have become friends as well as writing colleagues. The South Dakota state mammal is the coyote. This is appropriate, Amy writes, since the coyote is a scavenger, an apt symbol of our ability to survive whatever the Great Plains throws at us. The coyotes will be fat this fall from the losses of this storm.

Amy Kirk writes of the truths of the ranching life in the following stories–but she does not dwell on the tragedies and hardships. In these pages, you may not learn how very difficult it has been for her and her husband to keep their ranch running. Instead, you will find out why her wedding cake decoration walked off.

Her writing will make rural men and women nod with understanding, and it will educate folks who have never lived in the country. Knowing that some of the language will baffle some readers, she's even provided a handy glossary, defining such unfamiliar terms as "broken stem" (a bull's reproductive organ), "dry cow," (not pregnant) "hustle," (hurry up) "wrecks" (anything from a storm like this to being bucked off your horse) and "scours" (never mind).

I suspect Amy has been paying attention all her life, but her stories in this book begin with her marriage. Ranchers, she says, really get married so they have live-in gate-openers. She began married life in a house "slightly bigger than a large doghouse," a former Forest Service Ranger station. She was grateful it was modernized: there was one outlet and one light fixture in each room and a coal-wood Monarch range for cooking.

Immediately, Amy plunged into the realities of ranch living: one of which is that ranchers have to pay taxes but most of them don't like to do the necessary figuring.

What would she rather do than the accounts at tax time? "Pee outside in 30 below zero temperatures with the wind whipping at 40 miles an hour." Come to think of it, no wonder she enjoyed the blizzard this past weekend; the lodge where she was snowbound boasted indoor facilities! (So did my house; we melted snow to keep flushing.)

Amy's range of topics here is broad and intriguing. She discusses the colors of man food–white, brown and yellow–and reveals why men love beans. Why do ranch wives shave their legs–or not? How do you get your husband to take your advice? How do you change clothes in the hay field? Get in touch with your inner cowgirl? What's a cheap date for a rancher's wife during calving season? Amy answers these nagging questions about the realities of ranch life.

She considers the real difference between men and women to be obvious: "Men like beer and women like to make them feel guilty for drinking it." The reasons for this difference are too complex to reveal here, but chocolate is involved.

Writing of marriage, she notes that she assumed it meant sharing: he would use her guns and she could drive his pickup, but life is rarely simple. Still, the Golden Rule is always: Shut the Gate.

Ranch marriage usually involves ranch children, and Amy's skills at parenting are clear; she describes her Ranch Boot Camp as their preparation for real life. This, like so many of her topics, is humorous but with serious side effects. A rancher's work of land stewardship is all-encompassing, involving the behavior of his wife, his children, his pickups and farm machinery and even his dogs and cats. Whether the land on which the family lives is owned or leased, the rancher must care for it or lose his livelihood and his home. The rancher, Amy notes, must "think about livestock 24/7 365 days a year."

Ranchers are the original "upcyclers, recyclers, re-users, make-doers and get-byers." The modern movements by those who consider themselves "green" carries no surprises for ranchers, who have been practicing green living for generations—if they are still ranching. "Our cows have made us frugal and industrious," she observes. A rancher can "improvise his way out of" almost any predicament.

The dedicated reader will learn from this book why you should cultivate ranch wives as friends. For example, they carry jumper cables and know how to use them. They own and will loan to you large cooking utensils— crockpots, coffee urns, roasters— gadgets most families might not even consider until they're needed to supply funerals or weddings. Ranch wives can lift almost anything and they usually know a few things about plumbing as well. A ranch wife, Amy observes, is as useful as the "miracle wire" that holds most ranches together: old-fashioned baling wire.

Read on: and find out why Amy likes the cows she compares to Marilyn Monroe and dislikes the worthless ones she calls the Angelina Jolie cows.

–Linda M. Hasselstrom
Windbreak House Writing Retreat
October, 2013

Acknowledgements

Getting this book published has been an honor and a blessing for me. I credit the Lord's help that I have been able to achieve publishing this book and all of my writing goals. Through morning and bedtime prayer that God would bless my efforts and help me use my gifts for His purpose and to serve others, I have been able to find the column topics, the words, the wit, and the connections needed for readers to relate to my words.

To the people who believed in me, encouraged me, and supported me, I give my sincere gratitude. A deep-felt thanks goes to Adel Brown for giving me my wings to seek my adventure in the blue skies above as well as for her steadfast belief and encouragement in my words.

I've been fortunate enough to listen to Linda Hasselstrom speak and have participated in one of her workshops. She is not only a Custer County neighboring rancher and admirable woman, but a long-time inspiration to me as a writer.

To Marcia Hento, whose pursuits of her own dreams have inspired me to pursue mine with as much determination and whose encouragement and belief in my abilities and gift for writing have built me up.

Thank you to all of my wonderful and diverse girlfriends who have celebrated with me and cheered me on and to all the women I've met who continually amaze and inspire me.

I thank both of my parents Bob Studt and Martha Studt, who both loved and raised me, taught me valuable life lessons, gave me unique and varied skills, introduced me to different interests, exposed me to the outdoors, let me dream, and encouraged and praised me regularly. This book evolved from the childhood they gave me. Thank you for not giving me everything including cable television, but instead gave me the many wonderful experiences that didn't cost money and opportunities to use my imagination in overcoming challenges. To my siblings Clay and Jess, thank you for sharing in my celebrations and struggles along my journey.

To all of the newspapers that have carried my column. They took a risk on me and continue to publish *A Ranchwife's Slant* in their publications—people know my words because of newspapers' existence and readership.

A very special thanks to my publisher, Tom Moates, who believed I had something worth publishing in book form, who has been patient and encouraging from his first email contacting me, and who has allowed me so much freedom in producing this book. A big thank you goes to "Dr. Dave" Williams for copy editing my book and who so kindly and gently cleaned up my (writing) act and pushed me to stop being lazy with grammar rules and to strive to be a better, more polished writer instead. Thank you to Chris Legg for being tolerant in allowing me to make changes and decisions on my book's cover and layout.

To my family: Art, Myles and Reneé, for the times we've shared together joking and laughing at supper, working in the hay field, feeding or checking cows, and resting on Sundays when we could, and who have inspired many columns. I appreciate that they've allowed me to use some of our family's experiences for my column.

My husband deserves special recognition for being the man talked about and referred to in a lot of my columns. He is the king of our ranch and family life. Besides being my husband and confidant, Art is the man I admire most on so many levels regarding ranching, livestock production, fixing things, and getting stuff done. Thank you, Art, for being a man of your word, for tolerating my writing habit, and for letting me share with readers things about our ranching operation, daily life, family life, ranch mishaps, and our marriage, but also for sharing with me all your rancher insider tricks, secrets, and theories. I'm grateful for being allowed to write about all the things I love about you and for sharing things that many men in agriculture have told me they can relate to.

Lastly, I thank our cow herd, for always making my days ag-venturous, sometimes dramatic but always entertaining in the end. Their antics have faithfully provided me with fresh and unusual topics to write about.

Introduction

"Write what you know," frequently preached to writers, is the kind of advice I like to follow since I am most comfortable and confident writing about topics I have experience in: misinterpreting my husband's hand signals, following Murphy's Law, forgetting my husband's instructions, overestimating my expectations, and underestimating what cows are capable of. In my weekly column *A Ranchwife's Slant,* I often write about the cause and effect of ranch life regarding these subjects viewed from a mother's, wife's, or woman's perspective.

The act of writing has been a longtime enjoyment of mine. After my husband Art and I got married, I started journaling details of the big events that took place on the Kirk Ranch: our branding days, cow-moving days, sale days and calving season days. Initially it was my intent to journal a historical account of the experiences Art and I had while running his family's ranch. I began journaling more of my musings about the unexpected events in our daily life as a ranching family. Eventually these journal entries morphed into an outlet for me to decompress the good, the bad, and the crazy of our lifestyle. Or it could be looked at as a cheapskate's alternative form of free therapy when there isn't any fencing that needs to be done which always brings inner peace and clarity to difficulties and challenges.

What people unfamiliar with ranching are most likely to learn from reading this book is that our livelihood—essentially, the business of raising quality food that people will buy as well as to feed the world—is not for babies. Ranching doesn't just ask a great deal of physical labor from a human body, it demands it along with a lot of sacrifice, selflessness, doing without, making do, and being consistently inconvenienced in order to take care of our livestock's needs, which come before our own.

As a woman rancher, I constantly need to look for the humor amidst the unpleasant situations that arise while trying to co-manage livestock with my rancher husband. Anytime he's not around and I'm faced with a predicament, distracting myself with the search for humor regarding my dilemma has saved me from becoming irrational when needing to resolve a critical problem on my own. Looking for something amusing gets me through the tough days. When encountering a tank float not working and the water in the tanks critically low, a bunch of cows five miles outside the fence, a calf that doesn't seem to have the gumption to want to live, or a neighbor's bull (and sometimes not of the same breed as ours) in our yearling heifer pasture, having a sense of humor is a sanity saver.

Some situations have the ability to overwhelm me to the verge of having a meltdown or getting mad, but when frustration provokes me to cry, the wisdom of my Dad's words ring in my ears: "DRY IT UP!" If I can come up with something entertaining about my situation to distract my emotions, I'm more likely to get through my challenge rationally (once it's all over I can still cry if I want to).

What I do as a column-writing ranch wife is make myself vulnerable to reader head-shaking, judgment, and doubt. Most people would rather keep their faults, weaknesses, mistakes, and embarrassing moments on the down-low. I regularly expose those parts of our life, but I also like to think my columns shed light on what families really do on a ranch, not the propaganda that the manipulative media and radical groups make our livelihood out to be.

Once my column is on its way to print, I try not to look back or question my sanity about revealing the quirks and inner-most workings of our livelihood. It's always with the intention that maybe others can relate to something I share about my experiences or our family's that I justify telling on myself.

When I tell of our lifestyle's setbacks, demands, challenges or the work involved with people who have normal lives and jobs (the kind of lives and jobs that don't deal with animals numbering in 3 or 4 digits, have days off, vacation time, paid sick leave, and designated work hours) their faces say it all: "WHY?" Why would we willingly live such a life? The answer is simple: as every rancher and ranch wife will tell you. Ranching is addicting, which is why some ranch couples call it "a ranching habit."

Ranching's income is paid out in a lump sum once a year and our annual salary amount is contingent on things that are out of our control: the effects of the weather, the markets, the health and life of our livestock, and now, the persuasive propaganda that some people and organizations are using to influence, manipulate, and dictate the general public's beliefs about our livelihood and product.

Ranching is a lot of work, frustration, and minimal pay compared to the hours invested, and on days when everything goes wrong, we may get so mad we even ponder quitting. But we won't. The rewards are too hard-earned to quit easily and there's too much we love about what we do. We invest a lot of ourselves physically and mentally into our livestock's needs ahead of our own and we often feed and care for them better than ourselves. We worry constantly about them, regularly check on them, and provide for them with the best that we can afford (and sometimes what we can't afford), but some days the ranch work involved to manage them can be aggravating and disheartening. Doing our job gets frustrating when cows won't cooperate or don't understand that we're just trying to help them. And what do we get in return?—stories, memories, experiences, and life-lessons worth sharing.

The way I deal with a lot of the stress and problems I encounter when I'm by myself is with humor by imagining what my reactions might look like to outsiders. My imagination usually comes up with something comical and entertaining. Searching for humor helps me cope when faced with stressful moments: a bunch of cows out, getting the feed pickup stuck before having fed our cows, a cow that fights my help, or mechanical problems with equipment.

Being a ranch wife takes a special kind of woman, one who doesn't mind NOT having a lot of money, vacations, paid overtime, and sleep—when its calving season. A ranch woman has to have extra patience, tolerance, iron will, contortionist kind of flexibility (metaphorically), toughness, and calloused pride. I say extra because in addition to the normal amount of each that's needed for marriage, a lot more is required for dealing with a larger number of animals.

Sometimes I reveal more information in my column than readers might want to know about me, my family, our cows, or our daily life, but that's because I want people to know that my family and I are human. We do dumb things. Sometimes we bicker, yell, or cuss, and occasionally we get so frustrated that our temper comes out and we have conniption fits over stupid stuff. Part of the reason I expose myself to embarrassment by writing about the predicaments I find myself in is because I know how relieving it is to hear about someone else's problems and think, "For once, it's not me!" I want other people to experience that feeling on a regular basis and I try to provide that in my weekly column. The other reasons I divulge so much about myself and our lifestyle is because I may be desperate for a topic to write if it's close to my deadline and the only thing I can think of to write about pertains to my weaknesses, quirks, faults, mistakes, and my odd, womanly ways of solving ranch problems.

I've learned that if I don't find the humor in the things that happen to me, my husband and kids usually will, so I try to laugh at myself before my family laughs at me.

The realistic side of ranch life is that it's a messy, hard work-and-meager-pay business, but one that my family and I enjoy and are proud to be in. So with all that said, forewarnings given, and precautions assumed, let's get started with this ranch wife's slant about cowboys, kids, and ranch life. Are you in?

Ranch Country Language

The following is a glossary of some words and phrases commonly used in ranch country that will be helpful in reading this book. Ranch country language is similar to English but has room for misinterpretation. You'll have a much easier time understanding the language of ranch country and contents of this book by familiarizing yourself with the ranch country language.

[Swear Word(s)]: Exclamatory words and phrases used to imply frustration or impatience for any number of reasons. Meanings and interpretations vary depending on the circumstance and severity of the situation.

5, 6, or 7 Weights: Not in reference to the number of weights a calf can lift but abbreviated terminology referring to calves that have been sorted by weight weighing 500, 600, or 700 pounds.

Bottle Calf: Pretty self explanatory—a headache resulting from feeding a bum calf (orphan) a mixture of stinky powdered milk replacer with warm water twice daily, and having to thoroughly wash the bottle afterwards for what feels like a child's entire elementary years. A chore/responsibility commonly assigned to ranch children but sometimes pawned-off to their mother when school and extracurricular activities begin.

Broken Mouth: If you overhear two ranchers talking about their broken mouths, they aren't referring to the bar brawling days of their youth. They're comparing their old cows—specifically the cows that are getting old and starting to lose their teeth.

Broken Stem: A bull's reproductive organ that's been injured, thus rendering him unpopular with the cows, his services useless, and days of chasing cows over.

Bulling: A behavior identifying what a very anxious cow will do whose biological clock is ticking when a bull is around.

Butcher Critter: A sorted off yearling calf or two-year old that usually gets quite spunky anticipating its morning feed and is raised to be processed and packaged as a food supply into different meat cuts to fill a ranch family's freezer and hopefully last to feed the family for 9-12 months.

Calving: Assumed to be a no-brainer meaning either the act of an individual cow or a herd of female cows going through the birthing process to produce offspring during a specific time of year; typically springtime. You couldn't be more wrong. Calving is a sleep-deprived time of year, sometimes nightmarish due to harsh snowstorms in addition to daily and nightly checking, worrying, assisting, or bovine EMT responding to cows or calves, all of which can last for months. A season on the ranch calendar identified as a time of sleep deprivation and susceptibility to stress and worry-induced illnesses, irritability, and wearing-down, for the caretakers.

Cattle Pot: Not something that cattle poop in, but rather a large scale type of transportation specifically designed for livestock that cattle poop all over while being transported from a ranch to another location. And a little cattle pot jingle to go along with it: "Cows poop hot, cows poop cold, cows poop in the cattle pot nine days old," and then it gets really dried up in the pot. I may not have the words exactly right but it's some kind of jingle about green soup.

Chaps: A term with two totally different meanings and pronunciations. 1) (Pronounced *shaps*) leather legging outerwear worn by horseback riders to protect and/or keep their legs warm. 2) (Pronounced *chaps*) to become highly irritated—as in "*That really chaps my....*"

Cleaning: Referred to as a noun rather than a verb here. A gloppy substance expelled from a cow after giving birth to a calf (aka placenta) and oftentimes later accompanied by a barn cat or ranch dog chewing on it after a cow has eaten her post-calving fill. A substance frequently drug to a rancher's front yard also by the dog.

Disasters: Considered to be a big mess and can be one of several things: 1) defiant or uncooperative behavior by a herd during handling or while being trailed to a predetermined location, wanting to trail to a different location. 2) Discovery of partial or all cows in a herd that have caused a major problem such as breaking through a fence and grazing aimlessly. 3) A gargantuan problem that can potentially affect the whole herd such as snowstorms, herd illnesses, lack of water sources or forages, etc.

Dry Cow: There is the distinct possibility that a dry cow could also be thirsty, but in ranch country, dry generally refers to a cow that is no longer lactating.

Ear-tagged: A form of bovine body piercing.

Field corn: Not suitable for human consumption in third world countries as gullible, easily convinced people have been lead to believe by certain organizations promoting meatless diets, but rather a type of feed for herbivores which gets converted into food later, called beef that is suitable for human consumption.

Foot Rot: not to be confused with foot rot found in humans of developed countries, mostly the U.S., and associated with excessive walking during shopping, where people experience lameness in the feet from extensive mall shopping/walking. In ranch country, it's a type of lameness in cattle. Caused from inflammation of the skin, foot rot usually occurs at the cleft of a bovine's foot that's gotten infected due to a puncture wound of the foot or extremely wet conditions that have softened the skin, making the area more susceptible to infection.

Gather: to scatter in all directions or spread out via horseback or ATV. By doing so, horseback riders can search for cows in a large area. As riders find a few head of cows here and there, cows are pushed in one general direction, eventually merging into one large herd to be trailed someplace or brought into an enclosed area such as corrals for sorting, loading, or vaccinating purposes.

Get the gate: Means you. He's driving.

Ground Hay: A type of hay that does set on the ground, but in this case, it means hay that has been run through a hay grinder making hay easier for young cattle to consume.

Hired Hand: A rancher's wife who doesn't get paid to help him do ranch work.

Hole: Contrary to a void in the ground that people could fall into or should watch out for when walking, but rather a void needing to be blocked by a human barricade—usually a rancher's wife, sometimes a ranch kid, intended to keep cattle from escaping through at all costs.

Hustle: To move NOW; to move fast, with great speed; quicker than a super hero; often spoken by the rancher in charge who needs you to hurry over to a particular spot very quickly.

I Need Your Help for a Sec: A warning. A signal to be on high alert for irritable behavior and temperamental outbursts caused by frustration. A sign of possible trouble that you are about to partake in that has the potential to take several hours. A term that is used only when a rancher has been unsuccessful in doing everything possible to accomplish a task by himself and out of desperation, has come to the realization that outside help is needed in order to complete it.

Livestock: On the contrary, livestock is not a hot new aggressive investment, though livestock can occasionally get aggressive. Here, livestock refers to occasional chaos with four legs and a tail.

Makin' Bag/Bagged Up: Cows don't bother with handbags or make them but will show signs that they'll be calving soon by suddenly appearing udderly voluptuous due to their milk coming in prior to calving.

Open Cow: Readers may be compelled to think of a bovine that is open for a pass as in a ball game, but no, a cow that's open is not bred or her body aborted the calf too soon for some reason.

Pair: In ranch country, a pair doesn't have to do with socks, aces, or if you're a bad speller, fruit. A pair is a cow and her calf.

Pink Eye: Defined by ranchers as "pink eye"—an eye infection that affects cattle similarly to the way it does humans, but portrayed as foot and mouth disease to ignorant people by the propaganda of meatless diet-promoting groups.

Scours: See also "disaster," as it can become one, in addition to "bovine runny excrement."

She Cleaned/Hasn't Cleaned Yet: Cows aren't into doing any cleaning; in fact cows drop cleaning all together. Cleaned or not cleaned is referred to as whether or not a cow has dropped her placenta after calving; the timeliness this event reflects a cow's overall health.

Shipping: A nerve-wracking day for the owners/caretakers of livestock. The act of transporting a year's worth of hard work in the form of young livestock, usually to a sale barn, in order to collect a ranch's annual income which is determined by the bids of cattle buyers, all within a matter of minutes.

Slick Calf/Cow: A calf or cow that is NOT slippery when wet as one might assume by the word, but rather doesn't have its ID (ranch's brand) on him or her.

Slumped: Assumed to mean a cow with bad posture, but slumped in ranch country actually refers to a cow that has aborted her calf for some reason, causing the rancher to worry obsessively if other cows will do the same and how many, what the cause is, if it can be stopped, among other concerns.

Smooth Mouth: Has nothing to do with a rancher who is a smooth talker. Just that his cow's a gummer. She has no teeth. She's old.

Springer(s): Unlike bouncy cows, springers are cows that demonstrate or show signs of calving soon.

Stack Yard: A term derived from former days of harvesting hay the old fashioned way by stacking loose hay into a mountainous pile that was moved to a fenced-in area inaccessible to livestock. Although the term for the place where hay is stored is still used, the hay that is stacked is in the form of one-ton round bales neatly stacked in rows. The term "stack yard gate" has not changed, however. Wire gates to stack yards are still generally so tight they get called all sorts of expletives while being opened or shut.

Stem: An appendage that gives a bull a reputation for being a bovine Casanova; used for reproductive purposes.

Sucked: Not the most eloquent word in the language but nonetheless a status that is vital to a new calf's survival; abbreviation of the word "suckle," which describes whether or not a calf has sucked its mother's teat shortly after birth. A calf that has not sucked yet causes major concern with the caretakers.

Swather: What we call windrower and gets extremely boring to sit in and operate after a couple of hours, causing operator to become inattentive to what he or she is supposed to be watching for (big rocks, gopher mounds, broken section teeth) at times. Whether referred to as a swather or windrower, it is an agricultural mower that cuts swaths of hay, then spits it out the back in a windrow that's left to dry before raking and baling into a big round bale.

Wrecks: Abbreviations of disasters whereas cows do not read the rancher's mind in order to understand his instructions and expectations while being handled, and/or cows that do not cooperate according to plan and make a mess of a situation. Cattle behaving in such a way that makes a plan very challenge-filled and difficult to complete.

Part I:

Cowboys (and Ranchers and Farmers)

"I'm happy…things are goin' good. We're in between wrecks."
~Art, February 2002

Art and I getting ready to move bulls. (*Photo by Reneé Kirk*)

Ranch Marriages are Made in the Corral and Pasture

I know our marriage is not normal because most of our arguments take place in corrals or pastures surrounded by cows.

I have read several articles on surveys and studies on marriages that claim money is the main cause of arguments between married couples. That's not true in our marriage. Our biggest fights usually have to do with what my husband's hand signals were supposed to mean and what I thought they meant. Our other biggest fights pertain to a cow, a calf, or the whole herd.

Our idea of "marriage enrichment" or "marriage counseling" is to have lengthy conversations while checking cows. Not only is it cost-effective, we can cover a lot more ground this way, on our herd and on our relationship.

Running a ranch requires a very resilient husband and wife team. So much of a ranch couple's life overlaps that it's seldom we don't know how each other's day went or what's currently going on in each other's lives. Our work life, home life, and love life all overlap. It's not uncommon to celebrate Valentine's Day together dealing with an early born calf and having to get down on our knees in manure in order to get it to suck and fill its belly with life-giving colostrum.

Our marriage never lacks of excitement or adventure around here due to the unexpected events that arise. What makes our marriage different than that of the average

American couple is that in addition to making a home, raising up kids, having a dog, and going to work every single day, we add a cow herd to the mix. Something's always happening with cows and oftentimes needs both of us to deal with: a bunch of cows out, a neighbor's bull in, a fence down, water's not filling tanks, a cow has a backwards calf; the list gets long.

Cows are our guarantee that life and our marriage will never get stagnant. We may know what tricks cows can pull but they always find new ways to do them and know when to catch us off guard.

Going on dates or out for supper is a rare treat so we capitalize on doing things together such as work: feeding cows, checking livestock tanks and salt, and especially checking cows during calving season. These are the kinds of mundane tasks that ensure opportunities of unconventional couple time away from our kids on occasions when we give them the option of helping.

A few years ago I'd read about what husbands consider "romantic." Men enjoy doing "guy" stuff together with their mate and consider working with their wives romantic. After gaining a little insight into the male thought process on romance, I had a whole new outlook on helping my husband treat a cow with an abscess, pulling a calf from a cow in trouble, getting a sluggish calf to suck, pilling a calf with scours, or cleaning out all the calving barn stalls of mucky bedding and gloppy cow cleaning together.

The one true thing I can say with conviction about ranching as a married couple is that ranch marriages are never dull.

Ranch Life Puts Callouses on a Marriage

When my husband and I got married, it was a given that we'd be a dynamic duo. The matrimonial union between Art and me is comprised of a woman with a stubborn German streak and a man with a Scottish temper. Such a combination promised a life-long adventure. By including a herd of cows the livestock made sure of it.

The key to an exciting marriage is managing livestock together. Extremists such as adrenaline junkie-type ranch couples deal with just flighty, easily spooked young heifers or yearling calves, ensuring their marriage is always full of ranch drama.

> *"Did you know Amy married Art to fix things?"*
>
> ~*Myles age 5*

Cows provide all the elements necessary to have a marriage that's full of spontaneity, variety, and ample opportunities for couples to discover their mates' hot buttons. Cows make the conversations between couples more verbally vibrant and colorful and regularly add interest to the relationship between ranching husbands and wives.

Ranch life also provides a variety of activities that these couples can do together, typically referred to in the biz as "chores" or "work." Spouses who spend time together engaging in such activities on a daily basis quickly become calloused to any difficulties, hardships, and challenges in their marriage. Compared to a couple jointly managing a herd of cows, relationship issues are like a hangnail.

Husbands and wives whose work and leisure life revolve around livestock are among the toughest of couples. When a big problem arises on a ranch, spouses are compelled to partner up. Volatile markets, bad weather, and unruly livestock force spouses to become dependent upon each other unless one or both partners' moods are also unpredictable.

One key difference between couples who manage a livestock operation together and spouses who work at different jobs is that ranching couples witness what each other does at work. This minimizes gender gap issues common among other married couples. At the end of the work day, ranch couples can skip the "How was your day, Honey?" question. Working with the person you live with eliminates assumptions about whether your spouse is mad at you or is upset for some other reason when he or she gets home. If it's you, you know before you walk in the door.

Ranch couples don't have a lot of spare time and don't waste much of it arguing about problems in their relationship especially if there's a problem with the cows. Although I find that bringing up the past is kinda fun when our ranch life gets mildly boring and as my husband would put it, "We're in-between wrecks." By now I've covered just about every angle on our recurring arguments that I'm getting closer to permanently winning a few of our well-established ones.

Unlike for most couples, our biggest fights aren't about money. Ours usually have nothing to do with our relationship and everything to do with working together messing around with cows or my interpreting my husband's hand signals.

Regardless of the gender gap married couples sometimes get lost in, compared to the dilemmas of working with livestock and all the related problems that have to be figured out, dealing with a spouse is easy—you only have one of those to try to understand the behaviors of.

Art and I as newlyweds standing in front of our first home, dubbed "The Ranger Station." October 1994 (*Photo by Martha Studt*)

All Newlyweds Need a Ranger Station

When I attend weddings of young ranch couples, I can't help but think of the first four years my husband and I lived in the Ranger Station.

It was a cozy place where we felt newlywed togetherness and closeness because there wasn't enough room for either of us to have our own space. Every newly married couple should begin their marriage in a house like the Ranger Station—so named because it used to be one when it belonged to the Forest Service years ago.

The office building converted to a two bedroom, 1/16th bathroom home was slightly bigger than a large doghouse. As a new bride, I was very fortunate. The 1930's built house had electricity, just limited electricity. Each room was equipped with a two-pronged outlet and a light fixture.

Since Art bought the place from his grandparents before we met, the house was somewhat furnished. He had a couch set he bought at an auction, a kitchen table in the living room, and minimal furniture in the other rooms. The kitchen—some would call it a kitchenette—had a large boom box radio, microwave, refrigerator, and an empty Hoosier cabinet when I met him.

After he proposed marriage, Art moved the late 1940's black and white model *Monarch* range back into the house. The combination oven range came with "a complete *Monarch* coal-wood oven baking section" and was "equipped with four 'high-speed' electric units (burners) for summer kitchen comfort." Not being a cook himself, he had stored it in an outbuilding because he didn't have any use for it. Evidently he figured I would use it to heat the kitchen.

We were still living in the Ranger Station when we had our firstborn a couple of years later. During my pregnancy, it was really handy to have the bathroom only three steps away from the bed. Since space was at a premium when our son was born, baby paraphernalia took the place of any fine home furnishings, which were stored in the bunkhouse. With a baby in one room, our guest bedroom consisted of pulling out the living room hide-a-bed.

Surprisingly, our first home did have a central heating system. All heat came from the floor register's propane heater in the corner of the living room and kept our home cozy warm as long as we didn't shut any doors. When our son Myles learned to crawl, we built a "corral" out of child gates, the kind that fit in doorways, to keep him from getting burned when the heater came on.

The house's bathroom didn't have space for a bathtub and the kitchen didn't have room for a dishwasher, so I used the deep-sided kitchen sink to wash our son or the dishes, depending on what needed washing. It would have saved a lot of time, but I did not wash dishes and our boy at the same time. Luckily, by the time he outgrew baths in the deep sink we had moved to where we are now.

Newlyweds are deprived when they don't have an opportunity to live Ranger Station-style, where the best memories of their first years together are created. A couple hasn't been married until they've survived something together. And I'm not talking about losing cell service or internet connections. You don't forget being together with very little in the smallest of living spaces.

Humble beginnings make a couple tough and make for the best kinds of memories of a new life together as well as a deep appreciation for a spare room.

Junk Yard Wars

What's considered reusable junk is in the eye of the rancher or his wife. When I hauled home some stuff from our junk yard, my selected items weren't well received by my junk yard-managing husband.

Art and I have different opinions of what's considered worthy junk. He didn't see the decorating potential that I did in the metal buckets with holes, rusty bed frames, dry-rotted tires, grime-covered tool boxes, and bent, rusty rake wheels that I dragged to the yard.

Distressed-looking décor is really in right now, and since our outfit is well aged, brand new décor just doesn't fit in with the overall look of the place. I'm sure my girlfriends would agree that the resurrected junk I found would add charm to the place's overall appearance, although I'm still mulling ideas for the rusty bedpan I saw in the burn pile.

My husband didn't want the old bent up machinery parts that seemed like ideal conversation pieces and that I planned to incorporate into my flowerbed. I hand-picked junk I thought would add character to our yard but Art disliked my interest in the stuff he'd hauled away for a reason. He had a different vision than I did, one in which I took it all back to the junk pile. Their existence in the front yard was embarrassing to him, which I completely understood. His inability to visualize my junk's potential is similar to my feelings about some of his mutated shop projects.

What started my junk-hauling frenzy were clever ideas I found on the popular virtual pinboard site called Pinterest. Seeing what other people did with the kind of rubbish I've spotted in our junk and burn pile inspired me to retrieve a bunch of metal garbage for sprucing up the place.

"Mom, remember when Dad wanted to show me junk?" (go down to our junk yard)

-Reneé age 4

Since my husband's always telling me there's one of everything around here, I decided to go find some of them before he decided to haul off the good stuff and cash in on the scrap metal market. Due to my nonexistent decorating budget, a lot of our décor is either welded or hand-picked from our redneck Home Depot, the junk yard. There's an ample supply of décor there; all I have to do is add imagination in using it.

Being creative suits my decorating style because I like one-of-a-kind and unusual stuff and have found the best selection of oddities in our own dump. Old items that have been aged, weathered, and distressed, tie in quite well with my personality and our lifestyle.

Parting out old machinery and reusing scrap materials to build something useful for the ranch or to make existing equipment operable again is my husband's idea of good uses for junk. The stuff he's hauled to the shop, I would've considered car crusher worthy, and have made the grave mistake of saying so. The junk I suggested for a scrap metal cash crop my husband adamantly pointed out as renewable parts and resources for future projects—yet to be dreamt up.

Either way, Art can be grateful. My decorating style is a win-win for him. My choices for décor saves him money or makes him money because all those women on Pinterest who've caught onto the trend of repurposing old junk are helping drive up the price for scrap metal.

Marriage Tests

Once my husband and I surpassed our rookie year as a married couple, we began to see what really mattered in our marriage: figuring out and avoiding what annoys each other.

Details have always tested our marriage. I tend to include too many of them when I relay to Art about the chaos I faced handling a bull that got out, getting a near-dead calf to the barn with its belligerent mother close behind, the windrower getting plugged up while cutting hay, or numerous other problems I've encountered when he wasn't around. On the other hand, he doesn't use details enough to satisfy my understanding. He prefers getting to the point as quickly as possible. I like highlighting all the details on the way to the point.

Using details add interest to and heightens the ranch drama that I'm describing. Whether I'm giving Art particulars about cows I had to chase (or got chased by a cow), equipment breaking down, cows jumping over and/or breaking brittle fence wires, or stock tank floats not working, my storytelling builds up anxieties for Art as he waits to hear if the problem got resolved or still exists. Using as few words as possible pains me because doing so makes the explanations of my ranch chaos sound so boring and lame.

Art thinks details are for paying attention to. I don't pay attention to the little details nearly as closely, which oftentimes leads to regrets when he wants a follow-up. He'll ask me questions like how full the stock tanks were, how much salt is left, or much hay the cows wasted when I fed—details I don't always notice.

I like as many details regarding instructions as possible to avoid any misunderstandings. If I'm not given enough information to satisfy my confidence in understanding my husband's instructions, it raises too many questions and what-ifs, because I haven't mastered reading his mind the way a like-minded man would. Oftentimes I'll reiterate what he says which frustrates him and tests our marriage when what I repeat is wrong. His lack of information causes me to misinterpret his instructions. When he talks about "that gate at the Reed Place" (there are two) I can't be certain which one he means, but if he says, "That gate you hit with the horse trailer," then I know exactly which gate he's talking about.

Working together is the equivalent of a daily quiz in testing our marriage to make our work time pleasant. We each have our own way of doing chores and like doing them our own ways, but we also know we have to see each other at the end of the day and try to accommodate accordingly. Adding livestock or equipment to the equation is like a semester-final kind of marriage test. Balers that aren't tying, calves that aren't sucking, hay-cutting directions that aren't followed (or in my case, forgotten), bulls or cows that aren't in—they all put our love on the line.

Not listening or paying attention to each other has also caused rifts between us. There's a reason my husband looks me in the eye when he speaks to me—to make sure he has my full attention when giving me instructions or information that I'll need to recall later. Such chats rarely contain anything profound or interesting so I don't always commit them to memory unless he asks me if I'm listening to him while he's giving special instructions, but he does the same with my directives. If my directions don't pertain to a cow or a tractor and there's no picture of a turtle or rabbit (indicator of speed level on farm/ranch equipment) on the machine, he'll act like he doesn't remember how to operate the domestic machinery that I've demonstrated for him such as running the washing machine. He likes to give me the I'm-too-dumb-to-do-it routine instead because he's afraid I might expect him to do it more frequently or take over the job. Another test is when he doesn't complete a task the way I instructed, like loading the dishwasher the way I feel is most efficient in order to strategically cram beyond standard capacity. He thinks if he consistently does it wrong I won't ask him anymore.

Interpreting hand signals is a biggy that's always challenged our marriage. Some of our biggest arguments have been over a hand signal and what each of us thinks it should mean. What I thought was an inviting gesture once, turned out to be a hand signal to get out of the way. A lot of confusion could be eliminated if he would just communicate in my language—talking.

Fortunately, my husband and I have both studied enough to know what we need to review for our marriage tests. The reason we stand a chance at passing is because we're also good study partners.

A Cheap Date

There are two kinds of dates: the spendy ones and the post-marriage ones. I'm a cheap date.

My husband and I still go on movie dates occasionally, but during calving season our dates get cheaper. It's rare that we leave the place for any length of time unless it's to go grocery shopping or fueling up a vehicle in town. When we're cranky due to calving dilemmas, feeling overwhelmed, sleep-deprived, and in need of a breather, what we need is a date night. Since going someplace away from home is not always possible due to unexpected events with cows and calves, we oftentimes have to resort to improvising to go on a date; something ranching couples have to do a lot. Unlike those dates of old that ended at twilight, we choose to go out close to home before dawn.

The advantages to a cheap date are that nothing allows more alone-time away from kids than checking cows on a cold pre-dawn morning. Not having to find and pay for a babysitter is a perk to going on one of our cheap dates.

He picks me up promptly at the house, and I hop in the cow-checking pickup—a small flatbed pickup equipped with a roof-mount spotlight. We start with drinks: coffee in travel mugs. Instead of light coming from the movie theater's big screen, we enjoy the glow from the spotlight making three-quarter circle rotations back and forth across the calving lot. Forfeiting the aroma of hot buttered popcorn for the scent of manure and afterbirth isn't as appetizing, but that doesn't bother us.

At a movie, we know there's an unpredictable outcome. On cheap dates checking on cows, we know what the outcome will be, but the how and when of the outcome is the thrill of suspense: a set of twins, a backwards calf, a chilled calf, or a cow calving that wasn't calving earlier.

With cheap dates we don't have to be quiet as we do at the movies. We can talk about our date instead. We discuss things like what number is on a cow's ear tag, finding out if a new calf is a bull or a heifer, whether the cow we're spotlighting is one we should get in to the barn at daylight, and if a cow that still hasn't calved yet needs checked for problems. In between stops to record ear tag numbers of cows to check on later or that calved, we pick up where we left off in our other conversations that had previously been interrupted by our kids' demands.

Cheap dates are great—I don't have to find something to wear or fix my hair first, I don't have to take the babysitter home afterwards, but most importantly, my husband doesn't say, "I wanna make a quick stop to look at tractor I saw advertised for sale first."

Questions Are the Answers to the Gender Gap

Days or sometimes weeks prior to an all-family ranch chore like moving cows, my husband starts letting the kids and me in on the plan but only a little at a time.

He has this silly notion that when he shares what he wants everybody to do, he thinks he only needs to give us the man-version of the day's plan: explaining the plan with very little elaboration and few details for clearer understanding of his intent. As he explains what each person's job is, I try to visualize the scenario he's describing, and if I can't see it clearly I give him my "thinking" look. It generally leads to one of the few questions he'll ask of me: "You know what I'm talking about?" Then I proceed with rephrasing what I think he's talking about but I'm oftentimes wrong.

My first step in helping carry out any cow-related ordeal is to ask a lot of questions. If I don't think he gives enough information about how he wants to get the job done I start inquiring to fill in the gaps. It's just my nature; I'm a woman. My questions and rephrasing-his-plan sessions help me gather the information I need to complete my understanding because details are something he tends to leave out.

My standard procedure is to ask for more information than I really need about what he's thinking. I can always disregard what he says if it doesn't come in handy or isn't pertinent to carrying out my tasks, but I'd rather have more details than not enough. I've learned it never hurts to have an abundance of information once the crew splits up to carry out any task pertaining to cows or to meet a cowman's expectations.

Sometimes I ask questions even though my husband's already answered them because I either didn't pay attention the first time or I just want to confirm what I think his strategy is. Regardless, when he says, "I thought we went over this!" (meaning he thought I understood his instructions), I always use the excuse that his habit of mind-changing-up-until-the-day-of is the reason why I'm asking again.

Our crew leader will deviate from his original plan in the days leading up to a designated ranch job if a better strategy comes to mind. As a result, I have developed a bad habit of not fully listening to him until it's critical. The night before or the morning of are not good times for me to decide to pay attention. Starting up a conversation with a little review session to confirm the day's mission long after he's explained everything and assumed I understood, can be disruptive to his need for sleep, focus, and inner calm.

My asking too many questions causes problems in communication with my spouse. Not for me, mind you—I don't have a problem asking questions or asking the same ones more than once. Question-and-answer sessions distract my leader-husband from his focus, and they can cause him to wonder whether we understand what we're expected to do.

My husband may not understand why I have to ask so many questions, but the main reason is that it helps fill our gender gap.

Lessons From The NFR (National Finals Rodeo)

A trip to Las Vegas in 1998 for the National Finals Rodeo was an educational experience for my husband and me. May our lessons help other couples in planning their trips to the NFR.

Lesson #1: Get pre-conditioned to sleep deprivation, overstimulation, and being inseparable. My spouse and I weren't used to total togetherness, bed times extremely late, and nonstop activities. Be advised that within 48 hours of a shortage of sleep, tempers can flare up.

Lesson #2: Hold hands. In 1998, my husband and I didn't own flip phones—we left the bag phone at home. Holding hands might sound romantic, but we did it to keep from getting separated.

Our first Vegas fight took place surrounded by people at the Thomas & Mack Center. We split up to use the restroom before finding our seats for the rodeo, and when I came out I couldn't find my husband or see over the mass of people. There were black cowboy hats like his everywhere so I spent several minutes trying to spot him but he found me first. We were both so mad that what followed was a verbal collision over whose fault it was for getting separated and we didn't care who heard us.

Neither my husband nor I would back down long enough to acknowledge a young bachelor friend who approached us, for fear of losing ground in our argument of blame. Minutes passed while our smirking friend witnessed our bickering—amused I'm sure—before we finally stopped quarreling to talk to him. After that, my husband held my hand everywhere we went except for the trip home.

Lesson #3: After 3-4 days in Vegas, consider riding the elevator separately or choose a designated button pusher. What we call "The Elevator Story," is our most memorable Vegas fight.

I had our hotel's second floor button programmed into my head because we'd gotten used to getting off the elevator on that floor. By the third day I began to lose all concentration due to sleep deprivation and overstimulation, but even rummy-tired I could still push the second floor button like a trained monkey.

On day five we were in a hurry getting to the airport to fly home and needed to get off the elevator at ground level, but I automatically pushed the second floor button, and we had to ride the elevator through all the floor stops. Instead of keeping my finger away, my husband watched me push the same wrong button two more times so that the elevator kept bypassing the ground level floor for another round of stops. When it finally reached the lobby, my husband ejected himself from the elevator.

Lesson #4: The last lesson is to never leave your partner at the gate. My dawdling to get a coffee triggered our third dispute. While I was gone, our flight started boarding. My husband was considerate enough to wait for me, but when I returned, I knew leaving was a mistake. I watched our luggage take a beating as he quickly and carelessly dragged it down the steps to our small plane.

What we learned the most from our trip is that marriage is like an elevator. It consists of a lot of ups and downs. In general, it's a pleasant experience as long as the wrong buttons aren't pushed too many times.

One Man's Blind Study on Ranch Couples

Not long ago I picked up a worthwhile tip for enhancing marriages of ranch couples from a very intelligent and observant individual on the topic—a young bachelor rancher.

At a young farmers and ranchers conference where I spoke about communication between spouses in and out of the pasture, I shared some heart-warming stories (the kind that need an antacid) of my husband and me working cattle together. While enjoying the banquet dinner after my presentation, the young married couples at my table exchanged some of their own tense husband-and-wife cattle-working moments, which confirmed that my husband and I still fall in the normal ranch couples range. The bachelor seated next to me also participated in the conversation whenever the topic of cows came up. After listening to the different couples' spousal cattle-working stories, the wise bachelor spoke. He interjected with marital wisdom that I will never forget and couldn't help but agree with.

Through his various observations of married couples, he noted that the key to ranch couples' harmonious teamwork is based on, you guessed it, a good set of corrals. According to the bachelor's findings, he concluded that happiness among married ranch couples while working cattle together depended on the corrals that were used. My husband and I have worked in enough non-couple friendly corrals that we can attest to what your below-average corrals can do to a husband and wife's relationship.

You may not think of bachelors as marriage experts but it was clear that this single farmer/cattleman had devoted some time and thought to his blind study's hypothesis and findings. His conclusion hinged mostly on cows' behavior patterns in certain corral styles during handling and their effect on husbands and wives working together. There was evidence that while helping out on a friend's or neighbor's ranch, he had noted the resulting behavior patterns of married couples working in both run-down and good corrals. Most likely his conclusion was based on having to wait for the husband and wife team to finish squabbling before the work could resume, which is standard among normal ranch couples while handling cattle.

When getting cows to maneuver through or around corrals goes smoothly, efficiently, and quickly, harmony resonates between spouses. I instantly liked this guy's logic and wished my husband and I had his bank account. A good set of corrals like the ones he talked of and probably owned could solve all our problems except for the wayward-aims-at-the-toilet issue I keep bringing up to the males in my house.

It never really occurred to me that some of the quarrels my husband and I get into could have anything to do with our corrals and cows, and not him. I just always assumed that when cows balked, a cow got by, or a bunch scattered during a sort, it was my husband's fault and vice versa.

The wise man's conclusion on the root of ranch couples' cattle-working problems made perfect sense and I have since wished a long time ago that our outfit had the kind of corrals that eliminated our bickering. It's hard to say how many marital spats our friends and neighbors could have been spared, had a good set of corrals been in place to make sorting, loading, or running cows up the chute go easier.

As much as I enjoyed being enlightened on how to minimize marital arguments and agreed with the wise bachelor, it was apparent that this nice-looking young man still had some following-up to do on his study. Otherwise he would know that most normal ranch couples either can't afford upgrading with state-of-the-art corrals or they argue about them.

I Feel a Change in the Year

January and February is that special time of year ranchers start thinking about: taxes. Meanwhile, their wives are working on the taxes in order to be prepared to meet with their taxmen, but not me. I'm in pain.

As soon as the year changes I feel aches and pains in my back, neck, shoulders, and head, from leaning over the adding machine, receipt piles, and bank statements for several consecutive days, but my husband is very thoughtful in helping me overcome my seasonal pain. When my coffee cup needs refilled, pencils need sharpened, kids need disciplined, or supper needs made, he makes sure I haven't forgotten to include equipment we bought and reminds me about important receipts or anything else he thinks I might've overlooked to include. Aware of my headaches, knots in my shoulders and stiff neck, he'll gently and kindly ask me where I want all the receipts he's collected from the consoles of his pickups. He's very generous when it comes to giving me unfolded gas and feed store receipts.

When it comes to working on taxes, there are many other more enjoyable ways I'd rather spend my time. The first one that comes to mind is procrastinating, but I would willingly partake in any activity that's less painful than tax work, like spending eight hours in labor and delivering another 8 pound, 11 ounce child.

Working on taxes is not very mind-stimulating. I need activities that motivate me to move along, such as getting chased up a fence by a breachy cow or having a bull try to take me. Both would be more exciting than facing a pile of tax deductible papers and the blank tax booklet our accountant sends us to fill in.

If I had to choose between staring at the sun for half an hour or looking at tax-deductible paperwork, I wouldn't hesitate to blind myself. After staring at the sun, I wouldn't to have to look at taxes for a while. Similarly, if given the option, I would willingly pee outside in -30 below temperatures with the wind whipping at 40 miles per hour instead of sitting at a desk on a quiet, cozy afternoon indoors preparing taxes. The outside torture wouldn't last near as long.

> *"My head hurts.*
> *It must be tax day*
> *today."*
>
> *–Myles age 5*

Idle sitting for long periods of time gets to my hind end, but I would gladly sit through a two-day high school wrestling tournament without a seat cushion if it meant I didn't have to sit on a cushy chair to punch numbers on an adding machine and get buried in eraser bits. People-watching at tournaments takes my mind off the pain in my backside; working on taxes puts it there.

I'd rather dig out a vehicle buried in snow than wonder what we owe the IRS—digging out would be a more productive use of sweat. And I'd take stubbing my toe over stumping my brain on tax figures. A stubbed toe is worth swearing over.

Instead of thinking I was done and finding one more forgotten tax-deductible receipt that needs to be included, I would rather find a dead packrat frozen in a stock tank (which has happened to me) that needed to be removed. There are just too many other painful things I'd prefer to tackle than having to get taxes ready. Most of all, I'd rather just write about taxes than do them.

Applying Algebra to the Gender Gap

When it comes to the human species, only two things have been perpetually hard to understand: men's hand signals and women.

To all the men out there who get frustrated with their wives because they never understand or properly interpret your hand signals, I can relate. Let me be the first to welcome all of you to a woman's world. Women have always gotten frustrated that their husbands not understand how a woman thinks and, more importantly, *feels*.

The inner workings of a woman's mind are the most unsolvable mystery in the history of man. Since men's genetic makeup consists of 87% desire to figure out how things work (the remaining 13% consists of running the TV remote) all guys try to take a crack at figuring women out. It's in their DNA to accept a challenge.

Men continually ponder life's most pressing question about their wives: "How does she remember stuff I did to make her mad that happened during the Reagan administration?" Males remain baffled that women can change their moods faster than South Dakota weather. All men have come to the same conclusion regarding women's reactions to men's responses to the question, "How do I look?"—a woman's thought process is random. Men base everything on logic. Women can complicate the same exact thoughts with their so-called "feelings." In the male world this is known as being "too emotional."

Understanding a woman is nothing more than your average complex algebraic expression: it makes no sense, is difficult to understand, and frustrates every attempt to figure out.

Here's a sample algebraic equation of the average woman to elaborate my point. Solve the following equation:

$$(56 * 5 + 4) + [(12{,}107 + 562 + 3{,}235) - (842 \div 60 + \sqrt{1{,}369})] + (1{,}248 + 3{,}235) \approx [(a + b) * (15y) + 24(20np \neq 1 * 0) - (112 + 3y\, 3x + y + 2 \div \leq n) * \infty =$$

Since most men need a tutor to understand these algebraic expressions of women, my simplified explanation may help:

(56y) number of times a woman brings up something from the past, (5) times per year she leaves her purse someplace, (4) hours spent "getting ready" for a spontaneous date, (12,107) clothes combinations to choose from, (362) footwear, (3,235) outfits she'll try on, (842) times she says she has nothing to wear in (60) minutes, ($\sqrt{1{,}369}$) times she checks her derriere in the mirror during outfit changes, ((a + b)) times she can't find keys + sunglasses weekly, (15y) how often she says you aren't listening to what she's saying, (24) how often she gets mad when you try to fix the problem she shares with you, (20np) wants to talk about the relationship, ($\neq$) not equal to, (1 * 0) times you want to talk about the relationship, (112) how often she gets mad when she asks how she looks and you say flatly, "You look fine," (3y) number of mentions regarding your beer consumption, (y+2) unsatisfactory gifts you got her, ($\leq$) less than or equal to, (n) gifts you got right, (∞) how long before men will understand women.

To all you sister ladies out there, this is why men use hand gestures to communicate.

A Horseshoe Takes the Cake

After I tell people about the custom-made wedding cake top my husband and I had, they have to follow me to the gun cabinet to see it because that's where it stays now.

For our wedding cake, I wanted something western looking instead of the standard wedding bells or ceramic figurines of a bride and groom. It would've been too difficult to find a cake top that looked like my husband and me anyway. I would've been looking for a dark-haired groom with a big, Sam Elliott mustache, wearing a Stetson cowboy hat and western tie, and a blonde bride wearing cowboy boots. I also wanted a wedding day keepsake that wouldn't break so we could use it again at our 25th wedding anniversary.

I came up with the idea for our cake top and had my soon-to-be groom weld it. In order to do so, he needed a pony-sized horseshoe, one that had never been used, of course.

I explained what I wanted (think horseshoe on a stick) and before long he was showing me how our cake top turned out. He welded a metal rod onto a new horseshoe so it could be poked into the top of the cake and decorated with fresh flowers. The horseshoe seemed appropriate for the occasion since it symbolizes luck, and it fit in perfectly with our western ceremony.

After the wedding, I stored it away with the guest book, extra programs, and cake serving set, not expecting to see any of it for 25 years. Instead, I ended up digging it out after only a few years.

Our toddler son had become fixated with real guns and my husband and I decided it was time to lock the gun cabinet which meant we had to make it lockable. That's about the same time my husband asked me if I knew where our cake top was. I didn't bother to ask questions because I learned early on that he often got his inspiration from the most unlikely sources. After I dug out the cake top, he disappeared to the shop with it.

He was very proud of his solution to make the gun cabinet lockable and wanted me to see how it turned out. When I saw the new handles, they didn't look anything like what I envisioned so I asked him about the cake top. He pointed and said, "It's right there." He pointed to one of the cabinet door handles and the color drained from my face. I hadn't recognized my cake top in its new form.

His idea needed four horseshoes, and he knew the horseshoe on our cake top was the same size for matching one of the handles. Rather than waiting until he could get another one, he dismantled our wedding keepsake (gasp!) to use instead. I could hardly complain about it since he made the gun cabinet safe for our kids and put my mind at ease. I should have known though that if I used a shoe on my cake it was bound to walk off.

What Every Woman Needs to Know About Man Food

The way to a man's heart is by letting him enjoy his man food organically (aka nag-free) despite the indigestion he may talk about afterwards.

Any food-like substances or food combinations that women consider unhealthy or unappetizing, men are sure to love. Foods that contain the least amount of nutritional value make ideal man food choices. Men do not follow dietary guidelines. They prefer to go with their guts' recommendations instead.

> *"My stomach is durable. Except it can't handle mold."*
> *~Myles age 10*

To identify man food, wives should look for artificially flavored and preserved foods packaged to resemble something edible that doesn't need cookware to prepare. The best place to find such victuals is at the nearest convenience store. A lot of men headed to work will be swarming the heat lamps and microwaves to get their man food breakfasts.

Consumption in moderation is not something men bother with either. Bread is only as good as the half inch layer of butter, miracle whip, or chunky peanut butter smothered on bread slices.

Every guy's idea of man food may vary slightly but is typically the same: it comes frozen, in a can, or wrapped in plastic. Beer is a beloved man food also because wives don't like husbands drinking too much of it and makes the perfect man food combos like bratwurst brined in beer.

In order to eat certain man foods hot, a lot of men don't want to mess with a pan to cook it in. That's why grills and microwaves are man's invention.

> *"I'm hungrier than a coyote with mange."*
> *~Myles age 12*

Nutritionists suggest eating foods from every color of the rainbow but most man food derives from neutral colors. Green, blue, or purple foods aren't considered man food and are seldom eaten. Men's white food group includes milk, bread, potatoes, ice cream, miracle whip, and mayonnaise.

Brown man-foods include gravy, cooked meats, chunky peanut butter, candy bars, and pancake syrup. Then we have beans, which technically needs to have its own man-food group. Guys love all bean varieties: ham and bean soup, pork and beans, chili with beans, condensed bean and bacon soup, and cowboy beans—preferably from a can for quick preparation purposes. Man-food beans are what separate the men from the women. Beans are also many a guy's favorite because of beans' ability to be used as an excuse to act immature.

Yellow foods besides beer consist of Captain Crunch cereal, potato chips, and butter, to name a few. Then we have the yellow-orange category: processed American cheese slices. This cheese imposter is an odd little food men love to eat anytime. It's convenient, square, easy to fold and stacks up nicely for easy whole consumption. It may look nothing like real cheese, yet it is every man's first snack choice when he needs something to eat immediately.

The last basic food group of men consists of fast food, but not just any fast food; combo meals—the kind of food that's assigned a number for uncomplicated decision making. Unlike women's food decisions, which have to have certain exclusions and inclusions and adaptations, combo meals were created with men in mind and suit all men's need for simplicity at the drive-thru.

By now you've probably come to the same conclusion I have about the food men like. The things they like to eat are fit only for man so he doesn't have to share.

Our Marriage Rulebook

There's a reason why it's been said that marriage is a lot of work. It's because there are so many stinking rules.

Take my husband and me for example. We both assumed sharing everything was a perk to getting married. He'd get to use all of my guns and I'd get to drive his pickup. Neither of us realized that the other person had stipulations on their stuff.

His "rules for tools" established the earliest clause to our marriage the first time I used his wrenches. After trying half a dozen before finding the one that fit the bolt I needed loosened, I just returned them all to the general vicinity of the tool box. I didn't bother putting them back in order on the special wrench holder. My system didn't flatter him.

Similarly, I wasn't impressed when I found the brand new hand towels I'd set out for company, all crumpled and accented with a mottled, dingy-grey color. That's when I clarified the bylaws for cleaning up with kitchen and bathroom towels. Since then, it's been nothing but more and more rules regarding our stuff, creating an ever-expanding rulebook.

"A man's always gotta keep his tools handy!"
–Myles age 6

Most rules get established after something's been misused. His tin snips, for example, aren't for pruning lilac bushes, and my kitchen shears aren't wire cutters. His small folding saw for elk hunting, saws bones, not tree limbs, and my high-dollar kitchen knives aren't for cutting open plastic or cardboard packages. My vacuum and its attachments are not allowed to clean out old ranch pickups being traded in. My mixing bowls and wooden spoons can't be used for mixing milk replacer, and the kitchen broom isn't for sweeping grimy debris out of pickup boxes.

My husband's shop floor has to be swept clean if I make a mess, spill pet food, or scatter hay from the bale bed on the shop floor. I can't turn his cute pan for collecting motor oil into a planter or use his railroad ties for landscaping, and the see-through thin shirts he calls summer work shirts, are not to be ripped into rags, and he insists that if I have room spray in our only bathroom, it will save our marriage.

The rule on the freezers, pantry, and kitchen cabinets, is the same for pickup consoles and behind pickup seats. The person in charge of the appliance/ equipment will do the organizing, cleaning, and discarding—no matter how senseless the system and mess may seem. When encountering problems with each other's equipment like the windrower or computer, the same rule applies: DO NOT continue if you're not sure what to do.

We both have systems for doing things. He likes horse trailers parked a certain way (that'd be parallel and straight), and I like clothes slightly overlapping on the clothesline, not spaced apart. We don't hesitate to clarify our preferred way of doing things if each others' job details differ. And out of respect for each other's time, we follow rules. Each of us has to avoid unnecessary maintenance or cleaning on highly-depended-upon equipment like the tractor, rake, and windrower, or microwave, stovetop oven, dishwasher, and washing machine.

It's taken years, but we've learned the most important rule about our marriage. It isn't nearly as much work when we do things by the book.

Guilt by Association

The difference between men and women is obvious. Men like beer and women like to make them feel guilty for drinking it. This is because women feel guilty when they overindulge on chocolate and want some empathy.

- Men view beer as rightfully deserving at the end of a long work day. Women view chocolate as a "treat."

"Dad, when you got those cigars did you get a liquor license?"
~Myles age 10

Women don't want their favorite chocolate readily available. Instead they try to delay their indulgences by intentionally not buying it so they aren't constantly tempted. They'll also make deals with themselves by allowing occasional chocolate treats but will put a limit on how much or how often they can have it. If they end up eating more than they should have, they'll hide what's left in hopes of forgetting about it. Other chocolate-resisting strategies include making it difficult to get to, freezing it, and keeping it out of sight.

Men would consider this very stupid. Guys intentionally put beer in the refrigerator within sight and easy reach. They don't want to have to dig around clear in the back if they don't see it and don't like having to move stuff around in order reach it.

Oftentimes when women are trying to lose weight, they'll worry about overindulging on chocolate and offer to share it with a friend so they won't feel guilty alone. Men like sharing their beer with friends too while shootin' the breeze, but they want their friends to have their own cans.

Contrary to women's beliefs, men are concerned about losing weight. If the beer carton seems a little underweight, they get concerned. They'll also worry about whether or not there's any beer at home and will pick some up if there's any doubt.

When women eat more chocolate than they intended, many will feel temporary satisfaction, then chocolate-binging remorsefulness. When men drink more beer than they intended, many feel a powerful urge to take a leak.

In deciding whether or not to have some chocolate, women will drag out their decision. They'll mull it over by considering everything they ate earlier that day, analyze the pros and cons of having some chocolate, and if it's worth sacrificing their goal of dropping those extra pounds. Men don't put any effort into avoiding beer at all. They do not delay any more than is necessary if beer is on their minds or in their fields of vision.

It's been my observation as well as my personal experience that women will make a piece of chocolate last as long as possible. They'll try to savor it by consuming it slowly in several tiny bites. Men consume beer to drink it and savor it by having another. The only reason a man would sip any beer would be if it had a yucky flavor or nasty aftertaste, but even if skunky beer were all he had, he'd still drink it.

Men don't bother feeling guilty about drinking beer because they know it's senseless to worry about it if their wives voluntarily concern themselves regarding their mate's beer consumption. Women have more experience with consumption-guilt and do a better job worrying about men's beer drinking than men ever could, which makes drinking beer man's guilty pleasure.

Spouses in Translation

Some days I wish I were a cow. Then maybe I could communicate with my husband better and get the same attention our cows do.

I originally read the book *Animals in Translation* by Temple Grandin, about "decoding" animal behavior in hopes of finding out what a cow's got over me with my husband's attention. Cows seem to be easier for him to understand than me some days, but the book made me think about how my spouse and I are in translation sometimes.

For starters, since I talk and cows don't, my husband's other senses are sharper around cows because cattle are generally quieter. It's not unusual for my words to get translated into a language he doesn't understand during a conversation or argument. My talking seems to override his senses. Art and cows both notice little details and like a quiet environment, giving them opportunities to pick up on things in their surroundings. My excessive chatter can be too much for my husband to absorb at once and sometimes distracts him from effectively decoding what I'm saying, and my own words get in the way of what I'm trying to communicate.

Myles: "I don't think Grandma Mary was too happy with him (Art) as a teenager." Amy: "Why's that?" Myles: "'Cause he never tells anybody where he's going." (I was upset Art didn't tell me where he was going.)

-Myles age 12

Art spends a lot of time around cows and observes their behavior when he checks on them. He delivers their meals when it snows, makes sure they have a drink, and knows what, when, and how much they like to eat or what their diet is lacking.

He also dotes and spends money on cows because he knows their value and that the investment is worth the effort come fall. He takes them to new places year round and knows how to keep them happy and content. If he and I go someplace new, it's usually to check on the cows at the pasture we just moved them to.

He worries about the health and welfare of our herd and picks up on a cow's or calve's sign when something's wrong, then determines what it needs. When I'm sick, he'll check in on me from a distance so he doesn't catch whatever bug I happen to have.

Even though some of the cows aren't as young as they used to be, he still pursues them. If one gets mad and runs off, he'll go after her and bring her back. If I get mad and run off, he assumes I want some space and to be left alone. If a cow starts bawling, he listens and figures out what it'll take to console her. If I start bawling, he usually doesn't understand why and isn't sure how to react.

Sometimes I communicate silently and make a bunch noise instead to get my point across. When my actions speak louder than words, messages don't get translated any better if I slam cabinet doors, loudly clang pots and pans around, slap silverware on the table, and don't say anything. This behavior makes my husband vaporize from the room to a quieter place.

Regardless of how lacking my communication might be with my spouse, there's nothing left to say when we share an affectionate squeeze because hugs don't need any translating.

Love Letters Are a Chore

I've always teased my husband about his not writing me any love letters while we were dating. When our courtship was new, I was working on a fire crew that sent me to Arizona for three weeks. My pining for him led to my sending him letters when I had time.

I thought my ribbing had finally paid off when I went to the pickup to do chores one morning. He had to be gone for the day and I found a page-long note he'd written. "A love letter!" I thought. I was shocked because writing had never been his thing. While warming up the feed pickup, I began reading his words which started out with instructions. I'd asked him to write down as a reminder, the recent changes he'd made in the daily chores and I determined he must've decided to clarify those before starting his letter to me.

The next sentence contained more chore changes which I promptly skipped over. I was anxious to read the "juicy stuff" he'd written regarding our relationship: words of admiration, some appreciation, maybe a compliment or two. Instead it was just more instructions, which meant less gushing I'd eventually get to, and I got impatient. My eyes jumped down to the middle of the page and read on: "Feed the bulls buckets of creep by the barn door…push up hay…." I decided to review his instructions later and moved my eyes farther down the page to read what profound words he'd saved for last. "Feed what's on the pickup, then feed an orange twine alfalfa bale…." I read a bit further: "Load blue twine bale for the next day. Park pickup in the shop…."

Instead of feeling excited and sentimental, I started getting irritated. It was a kindergartner being told by the teacher to close the lid on the glue bottle so it wouldn't dry up, kind of letter.

Once I reached the end I decided maybe I should re-read it again but slower. I started a third time thinking if there was anything of value to read, I could have easily overlooked it, and searched for key words that could be interpreted or twisted around as affection, admiration, or sincerity, but I still didn't see anything flattering. The closest I came to having my breath taken away was feeling flabbergasted that he'd written enough to fill a sheet of paper.

What he'd written was just a page of instructions, and I was aggravated for thinking it would be a rare love letter. After doing the chores that morning I decided to go dig out my keepsake box full of birthday, anniversary, and Mother's Day cards he'd given me over the years containing special sentiments and re-read through all of them. I'd saved all the cards he'd ever given me because they were the only times he'd written something that resembled a romantic love letter. Each card had at least one sentimental sentence he'd written.

His handwritten note full of reminders and changes to the daily chore routine wasn't what I'd expected but I got over it when I realized that if I put all the sentences from each card together, they'd fill up more than a page.

His page-long chores list may not have been the love letter I was expecting but at least he wrote down what he wanted me to do. His hand signals are a LOT harder to figure out.

Getting ready to bring the bulls in on a snowy day. (*Photo by Reneé Kirk*)

The Ranch Wife

The level of importance that the ranch wife plays goes much deeper than being supportive and encouraging to her rancher and their lifestyle. Ranch wives do a lot of behind-the-scenes work.

It's the ranch wife who takes care of the little underappreciated jobs like holding a cow's dirty tail out of the way for her husband when he's working on a cow whose calf needs to be pulled. It's the ranch wife who accepts the job of massaging an unmotivated baby calf's goopy poopy butt to replicate its mother licking its hind end so as to stimulate the calf's urge to suck, while the rancher guides the calf's mouth onto a teat. It's typically the ranch wife who washes the foul-smelling milk replacer bottles, nipples, and vaccine guns in her kitchen sink. It is the ranch wife who is specially picked (because no one else is around) to block a gaping hole with only her body and a sorting stick to keep bulls or a bunch of skittish heifers from wanting to go through it. And, yes, it is the ranch wife who rakes hay with the old open cab tractor on a hot, cloudless day because the upgraded and air-conditioned tractor is hooked up to the baler following behind her (okay, so it is also because her husband might suffer from hay fever).

When a ranch family is moving cattle, the ranch wife is always there helping with sorting in the corral or trailing cattle on horseback while at the same time she knows where her kids are at and what they're doing—or at least what they're supposed to be doing. She's the one who changes the cowkids' dirty diapers on a pickup seat, thinks ahead to bring everybody snacks, water, and lunch for the hungry cow-moving crew (at our outfit that would be my husband, our kids, and me). At the end of the day when the ranch work is done, it's the ranch wife also provides a hot meal for the family at suppertime.

The ranch wife is highly relied on to bring out lunch or a fresh jug of water to the hay field, and runs for parts, fetches tools, goes after forgotten items, or gives rides back and forth to get machinery moved because she is knowledgeable, dependable, of legal driving age, but more importantly, she's always there. The ranch wife is the go-to person (usually because she's the only one around) her rancher calls on to start the tractor when he hollers, "OK, NOW TRY IT!" or when he asks, "Can you come help me for a sec? It'll only take a minute," even though realistically, those are the words that always mark a job much longer.

When you visualize an American ranch, be sure to include an image of a ranch wife getting a gate to make it accurate because that is an iconic scene of today's ranches. I shudder at the thought of what would become of our country's ranch life if ranch wives weren't around to get the gates.

Monday Mornings Are Special

Unlike most people, I consider Monday morning to be special. It's a weekday that means something unexpected will happen; a day that frequently fulfills my fondness for surprises.

> *"If you wanna be me, you wouldn't wanna be me now."*
>
> ~Myles age 10

I typically experience my "ag-ventures" on Mondays. The prerequisites to an ag-venture are that it has to be unexpected, pertain to agriculture, and be an adventure. My most memorable ag-ventures have all happened on Mondays.

I recently had a doozy ag-venture mostly because I was long-overdue. It was the dawning of a bright, crunchy (due to dried up grass) August Monday morning before 7 a.m. I'd offered to check water tanks out on the range because my son and husband wanted to leave early to go to Rapid City, South Dakota on a pickup shopping trip for my son.

I decided to get an early start since I had arrangements to be in Custer mid-morning. I loaded up our dog in my jeep and hit the dusty road. Pepper and I were enjoying the change from our standard morning routine (taking care of our replacement heifers' water) as we jounced happily along listening to the radio. Several miles out on our route the jeep suddenly died, and immediately thereafter, panic set in. The first thing I said at the sight of smoke coming out from under my dash was NOT, "Oh look, Pepper, there's smoke coming from the dashboard of my beloved jeep! I wonder what's going to happen next!"

I quickly shut it off, fidgeted with hood latches and lifted the hood to assess the problem. I first had to gingerly move some melting wires and being the woman that I am, I determined absolutely nothing. My jeep could not have chosen a drier, more forested area had it decided to catch on fire while in the midst of a high fire danger. All I had to put a fire out with was less than a quart of coffee and a forgotten-about down-filled coat stuffed in the back. Luckily the jeep decided it only wanted to die on me.

After confirming that the jeep was not going to ignite and start a fire, I cranked the steering wheel to turn and back my jeep off the road. I did this repeatedly, since Pepper did not want to cooperate and steer for me. Not knowing how long it would take to get home, I put on the backpack I'd brought along and filled it with stuff I didn't want left behind and prepared to jog in order to make it home in time to carry out my plans in Custer. I headed in the direction of the next stock tank since I guessed it was along the shortest route home but got a little resistance from Pepper about jogging. She looked at me as though I was daft for not getting in the jeep to leave, but she soon got sidetracked sniffing around and marking new territory along the way.

This kind of adventure would cause a normal person to curse Monday, but I always look at the positive. As sweat rolled down my temples and soaked my back I noted that not only was I getting three miles of exercise in but more importantly, this "Monday Morning Special" was a nice change from all the others. It didn't involve having to deal with errant cows.

(FYI the jeep's battery had come loose and touched the firewall causing it to short out.)

Time to Change

The hay field may not be the first place people think of for making changes in their habits, but one particularly frenetic haying season forced me to do a little changing.

My husband and I had been trying to get a couple of fields raked and baled before it either got too dry or too rained on. Around the same time, a girlfriend was in a bind getting her summer rental cabins cleaned and asked if I could please help her out in the morning. I agreed to help her out and promised Art I would show up around noon to take over the windrowing so he could rake or bale.

I wore my cutoff shorts, a tank top, and flip flops for cabin-cleaning comfort and brought my hay field work clothes along to change into afterwards.

I arrived at the hay field at noon as promised, but was running late getting there, so I didn't get a potty break or chance to change clothes beforehand. When I got to the hay field the windrower was at the other end of the field, giving me plenty of time to take care of my restroom needs and change my clothes. Wary of being seen by cars going by, I hid behind the pickup and out of sight of the highway we were haying next to and quickly got my clothes changed before any cars could see me. By the time I got changed, the windrower was headed in my direction.

While I stood in line with the windrower waiting to take over, I noticed something different about my husband. As the windrower got closer, I was able figure out what it was: I had just given our bachelor neighbor an unintentional strip show.

As my luck would have it, our neighbor had asked Art to do some welding on his broken rake and had offered to take over windrowing until I showed up at noon. Needless to say, I hadn't gotten the memo.

I have many personal habits I should be doing differently, but while I'm waiting for the windrower is not the time to change.

Ranch Life Suits a Gemini

I've never been one to read or put much faith in my daily horoscope, but from what I understand to be my Gemini traits from the little bit that I've picked up over the years, ranching and my so-called Gemini characteristics are perfectly suited for each other. Both are chock full of the unexpected, and our unpredictable lifestyle is well-matched to my mercurial nature and penchant for adventure.

Work on a ranch takes place outside and requires a lot of physical activity—a Gemini's dream work environment. Without large doses of sunshine, the outdoors, physical activity, new challenges, and change, days can feel like slow death. Long-standing routine and drudgery kills a Gemini, but ranch work and chores that change with the seasons make for a job that's almost as exciting as working with the unpredictable cows that make up our chores.

Similar to life on a ranch, life with a Gemini is never dull. When my husband gets impatient trying to find the pitchfork, the twine cutter for cutting the twine on round bales, or the binoculars and spotlight for night checking cows during calving, he'll ask, "So where'd you leave it *this* time?" It's most likely in the vicinity of wherever I used it last and I seldom pay attention to where that was. I distract him with my sign's trait of cleverness, wit, and charm while I try to find the sugar or butter for him by responding, "That's my contribution to keeping your life interesting and my reassurance that you'll think of me regularly, Honey."

Whether Art realizes it or not, when he proposed to me he also made a very wise business decision. Not only do Geminis love learning new things, we are highly independent, multi-faceted, and self-starters, renowned jacks-of-all-trades which is invaluable on a ranch. He also likes people around who can hustle when helping, which Geminis excel at; we're often characterized as being quick and mercurial.

Being married to a Gemini has also spared my spouse the expense of time and money in getting help with cows, putting up hay and doing other ranch-related tasks. Versatility enables Geminis to do several different jobs, which is exactly what ranching demands. We can handle whatever is required of us because we're like chameleons: changeable to any situation. My husband prefers not to waste a lot of time explaining or supervising and knows I understand (the majority of the time) what the day's mission is and trusts me with all of the old equipment. Once I get the gist of something, I can handle any job assignment and I do my best work when unsupervised.

Art never knows what's in store when he leaves the house or comes home. In addition to cows and equipment that periodically create surprises with new situations that baffle him at first; he also has to contend with South Dakota's weather patterns. Our state is notorious for not following weather forecasts, being erratic, and having temperature changes that switch from one extreme to the other within 24 hours. Likewise, I am constantly putting my creative and inventive mind to work on home and ranch projects or on resolutions to ranch problems in ways he never would have imagined.

If times get really tough, he'll never have to worry about me abandoning him. I'll always be the last one to consider jumping ship. I would hate to miss the adventure of riding out any storm. Adversity and the unknown give Geminis purpose.

Once, we experienced a five day power outage from a snowstorm, and when the electricity was restored, I was secretly saddened. Difficult times motivate me to strategize ways to help us cope. I counter Art's sometimes despondent nature at the onset of a hardship with my optimistic outlook. When he gets stressed from problems sandbagging us all at once I tell him not to worry, having a Gemini around is a good sign.

Getting In Touch With Your Inner Cowgirl

When any of you ladies out there get to feeling out of control, in a rut, downtrodden, or run over in the rat race, take the time to restore your soul and get back on your feet by getting in touch with your inner cowgirl:

- Take the back roads and savor the countryside.
- Skip the hair and makeup routine for a day. Wear a ball cap or a visor.
- Use duct tape for repairs.
- Drive a stick shift vehicle or a pickup for a spell (NOTE: it's not a "truck" unless it's a one ton. Pickups are ¼, ½, or ¾ ton outfits).
- Play cards: Poker, Blackjack, Gin, Cribbage, or Texas Hold 'em.
- Spit—but practice first. There's an art to spitting without having drool dangling from your lips.
- Belly up to a bar, down a domestic beer, and eavesdrop on men's conversation. See if you can learn something new about the male species, or better yet, join in on their conversations.
- Trim your fingernails short. See how much more useful you can be without manicured nails, and then put some calluses on your hands.
- Carry a pocketknife.
- Change a tire by yourself or use a set of jumper cables.
- Save time, money and water, and ditch washing your vehicle for a month. The dirt makes a great surface for drawing a map or a heart on.
- Wear something made by Carhartt: a jacket, vest, coveralls, bib overalls, or a cap. (There are other colors available besides duck brown.)
- Sink your teeth into a juicy hamburger served on a buttery toasted bun or swig a cup of coffee at a sale barn cafe. They serve the freshest, tastiest burgers and coffee around.
- Spend a day horseback appreciating nature, the earth, weather, animals, and most especially, the quiet.
- Buck up.
- Avoid going to town or spending money for anything other than groceries and personal items for a month.
- Volunteer at a farm or ranch for a day doing manual labor chores: pitching

"Arm holders" (bra)

~Reneé age 3

"I was always wondering about bras. Why do girls wear them?"

~Reneé age 5

hay, filling feed buckets, chopping ice, packing salt blocks, cleaning stalls or handling livestock and see how accomplished and good you feel afterwards.

- Observe livestock. Get to know the animals' behavior. Spend some time quietly listening to and watching them.
- Pull a calf from a heifer that needs assistance calving or hold down a calf at a branding.
- Eat rocky mountain oysters cooked on a branding stove.
- Replace your packet of tissues with a bandana.
- Watch *Lonesome Dove* or read the book, or do both.
- Get seats at a rodeo close enough to get some arena dirt in your lap and feel a breeze from a horse loping past you.
- Get fresh air into your lungs and enjoy a good night's rest by working outside all day or spend a summer night sleeping under the stars listening to all the sounds that nature provides.
- Learn the lyrics to a Chris LeDoux song.
- Help check, fix, or build fence all day and let your mind empty out.
- Don't complain.
- Work in the dirt, mud, manure, grass, and/or with greasy equipment and get your jeans dirty.
- Wear cowgirl boots for work, play, and leisure for a week.
- Be neighborly.
- Keep a wad of baling wire and roll of duct tape handy to use the next time something needs fixed.
- Groom a horse for 20 minutes instead of yourself.
- Get outside and watch the sun rise, the sun set, or the stars blink at night.
- Savor an afternoon siesta on the ground on a sunny day (ideally, in spring or summer).
- Listen to a playlist of songs fit for cowgirls. Start with some of these: *How 'Bout Them Cowgirls, Even Cowgirls Get the Blues, Amarillo By Mornin', Mamas Don't Let Your Babies Grow Up to be Cowboys, Whatcha Gonna Do with a Cowboy, Cowboy Logic, What the Cowgirls Do, That Girl is a Cowboy.*

Getting to know your inner cowgirl is easy, but to find the real cowgirl in you means you'll have to pee outside.

Work Mess Code

At different times in the past, I have held short-lived jobs requiring dress clothes. Picking out different outfits for inside work was by far the toughest part of those jobs.

Making a decision on slacks and tops everyday was no Sunday picnic for me, and I quickly developed withdrawals from my jeans and sweatshirt comfort. That's why the clothing attire for ranch work is a dress code well-suited for me. Job descriptions around here require what I call comfort and practicality career wear but is probably viewed by others more as the grunge look from the 90's. The grunge image incorporates rough-looking and well-worn flannel, faded denim, and hooded, quilted plaid flannel jackets, which I've always worn in the winter anyway. I also have sweatshirts turned grunge from so much wear and washing.

I like work wear best once it starts showing a little age: well broken-in with all-day comfort appeal. Since our household is big on water conservation (mostly out of necessity) I don't wear a different outfit every day. Only after a few repeat wearings of the same jeans and sweatshirt do I pull out a fresh set to wear. Perks to this wardrobe are that I don't freak out when coffee dribbles down the front of my shirt or I accidentally swipe my pant leg against a muddy pickup.

The only criteria I expect from my work clothes is that they still fit and serve the purpose of keeping me protected from the elements, depending on the season. "Best-dressed" around here means most well-equipped for the job and weather. I can change up my same outfit a bit with my brown coveralls, chore coat, lace-up overshoes, or work gloves. I also go for the layered look in cold weather with long johns, t-shirt, hooded sweatshirt, and jeans with frayed holes at the knees.

Regarding footwear, the nastier they look, the better. The more wear, duct tape, mud, and manure on a pair of boots the more respect. Work boots represent the level of hard work someone does or how high maintenance a woman is about getting dirty. Anybody wearing clean or new boots will likely get razzed.

Part of the grunge look is appearing disheveled, which I excel at. I extend the grunge image by putting up my long, stringy, uncombed hair in a ponytail and wear a visor or ball cap. Like other grungers, I also prefer an un-tucked shirt due to its less-hassle appeal. It's pointless to tuck a shirt in when my bladder can't hold a pot or two of coffee for very long (definitely a drawback for women in coveralls).

Going grunge is not an impressive appearance, but I don't have to impress anybody around here, nor have I ever. During the winter, cows don't care what I look like when they see me bringing them hay.

I may not work where dress clothes are required, but I still experience outfit anxiety. The amount of time I spend deciding what to wear when getting ready for Sunday church is a mess of work.

My former family car, a Ford Explorer SUV, converted into a ranch pickup, loaded with a four-wheeler and ready for ranch work. (*Photo by Amy Kirk*)

Redneck Mother's Day

Of all the Mother's Days I've been fortunate enough to have, my most memorable one isn't recalled with fondness. It's known as my "Redneck Mother's Day."

Most years, I let my family off easy because I help out every year at my girlfriend's flower shop the busy week prior to Mother's Day. By Sunday, I'm usually so wiped out I don't expect too much for Mother's Day. Just a special card, gifts the kids made at school, or the family doing my housework is enough for me.

One particular Mother's Day started out like all the rest, with me being the first one up and everybody going to church. The children's lesson about remembering Mom had quickly worn off as I listened to backseat bickering on the way home, so to stay calm I focused instead on recalling the sermon about praise for mothers.

I didn't lose hope though, as half the day still lay ahead, and I was sure my family would come around for me. When I mentioned Mother's Day wishes like someone doing my household chores, everybody scattered like barn cats, and I got an excessive amount of "alone" time instead. With the house all quiet, I took to napping on the couch until I was abruptly awakened mid-slumber. My son and husband hollered from the kitchen door, urging me to come see their shop project.

Since I had anticipated the day to be a Mom project instead of a shop project, I didn't share in their excitement. After being bothered repeatedly, I was certain I wasn't going to get a decent nap until I went to see their surprise. I walked out to the shop sloth-like, while my son hopped and skipped around excitedly like a monkey waiting for his banana, anxious to show me what he and Dad had done.

Entering the shop was like standing by a flag pole humming during a lightning storm. The place was juiced with high-voltage testosterone pride. What sat before me was my boys' version of *Farm Show* magazine's latest "made it myself" idea, a ranch-style convertible. With the help of a welding torch and duct tape to cover sharp edges, my husband and son had converted my old Ford Explorer SUV family car into a small ranch pickup/four-wheeler hauler.

They tried to impress me by pointing out all its finer points but couldn't understand why I didn't share in their enthusiasm. I expressed my disappointment in not getting my family's undivided attention for just one whole day. My husband's quick-witted response was, "We just thought you wanted some time alone!" I wasn't sure what they were expecting my reaction to be, but after acknowledging their convertible, I went back to the house for the "alone time" they thought I wanted so badly. They got the vibe with my body language and facial expressions that I wasn't impressed as much as they were. Later, they made me to take a ride in their ingenious, one-of-a-kind SUV convertible to make up for their unapproved shop project and had me laughing about being the only mom to go on a Sunday drive redneck-style.

I couldn't say they lacked creativity in surprising me and I still tell my family I like being surprised for Mother's Day. It just can't involve a welding torch, duct tape, or bailing wire.

Job Security

It's highly unlikely that I will ever find myself out of work. My chances of getting fired or let go are slim. Trust me, I've tried.

My position would be hard to terminate or outsource because I've made the mistake of creating a job for myself that nobody else would want. Since my position is customized, it's well-relied on around here, but it is basically useless anywhere else. I have more than enough to keep me busy helping my husband manage our ranch chaos.

I've juggled everything from plumbing problems like being out of water to discovering unexpected issues with cows just as I'm leaving for an appointment. Working here may provide plenty of variety but not the kind most people would appreciate. Some days I deal in manure, cookie dough, or bread dough—but not simultaneously, mind you. Other times I work around afterbirth and milk replacer, or if it is summertime, I have to deal with bits of hay poking me in unusual places, tractor grease and my jeans getting ripped on barbed wire. It all depends on the season.

Amy: "So what did you do at 5 a.m.?" Myles: "I did what you do." Amy: "What's that?" Myles: "Dink around with my stuff."

-Myles age 8

My career, if you can call it that, is greatly influenced by my husband so there's not much of a demand for what I do, except to him, our kids, and our cows. He prefers lining someone out who understands what he wants done and who knows what his expectations are. I usually don't, but I'm good at faking it. Art has always expected a lot of man-work out of me after I made a special effort to prove that I could do heavy duty labor during our courtship by telling him about working in the woods with a chainsaw and firefighting at my Forest Service job and being his calf-wrestling partner at brandings. A few months after we started dating, he proposed, and a year later we married. Part of my occupation now involves doing hard labor that some young men can't even do.

Another reason my "job" is at low risk for being replaced, downsized, or phased-out is because most people are looking for something with a benefit package and wages. My position is what you'd call "in-sourced;" doing what other laborers would normally get paid for doing.

Art also knows it wouldn't be cost effective to eliminate my job. He doesn't have enough time in years to re-train someone else to do everything I take care of or the patience to start over explaining his hand signals. Another reason he wouldn't know how to train a new person for my position is because he only knows half of what I do. The other half pertains to the non-ranch related work I'm in charge of doing: laundry, cooking, cleaning, grocery shopping, household managing, and kid schedule wrangling.

It's also safe to say that my career isn't in jeopardy of being downsized as a part of any budget cuts. For the duration of our marriage there's never been a pay scale since there's never been a budget for what I do.

Besides a minor thing like money, my career as a go-to gal for home, family, ranch chores, and livestock provides me with all the things I need: a job, room and board, a family, a sense of humor, and every now and then an opportunity to get a new pair of work boots and blue jeans.

Hung Up on Pickups

Back when I was still playing the dating game, I heard plenty of pick-up lines. Some were clever, others were desperate attempts, and a few made me walk away.

Pick-ups that made me exit the area quickly were guys saying something like, "Wanna take a drive in my truck?" while looking over at his half ton. Mentally, I was saying; "Go back to school and study up on your vocabulary words before asking me out. Pick up a dictionary and look up the word 'truck.' It clearly defines what a truck is." I figured all guys knew the difference.

Misuse of the word "truck" and people referring to their miniature, half, or three-quarter ton pickups as a truck happens to be a big pet peeve of mine. It annoys the H-E-double toothpicks out of me. Most of my pet peeves usually have something to do with my husband's or kids' habits, but this one ranks right up there with OCD (obsessive-compulsive disorder) kind of annoying.

"It sounds like a semi-truck." (church organ)

~Myles age 5

Maybe it's just the way my husband and I were raised, but we both agree that a pickup is defined as a utility vehicle weighing less than a ton. Pickups are for "picking up" things, you know, like lumber and cattle panels.

I even researched our theory by going straight to our library to confirm the validity of our theory against the phenomenon among Americans who insist on calling their Ford Rangers and other light duty vehicles "trucks."

In the chunky book section for toddlers, I found the one titled "Trucks" in tall letters. It was beautifully illustrated with big photographs of actual trucks: Dump trucks, semis, fire trucks, tank trucks, logging trucks, and refrigerated trucks. Clearly, trucks are just "heavy duty" equipment that hauls stuff. The book labeled each picture using large print to spell out each kind of truck for easy reading and understanding. I carefully looked for a picture of a pickup. Amazing, there it wasn't. I put the book back on the shelf and all doubts aside.

I refrain from correcting people when they talk about their half ton pickup as their truck but it's HARD, really hard. It's a real nerve getter for me and probably very few others, but when people mention their truck, an eighteen-wheeler sitting in their driveway comes to mind, then I do a mental correction of the misuse of the word.

At the repeated offense of the term "truck" to mean pickup, I have to refrain from starting an argument. The irritation gets worse every time people refer to what is clearly a pickup, or in some cases, a Tonka toy pickup on steroids. The opportunity to correct these people is there, believe me, but I can't bring myself to say anything about it. I really want to set "truck" users straight, but I don't. Instead, I go home and vent with my husband about another instance of "truck" ignorance.

I've determined it must be a case of adult peer pressure because other men and women are saying "truck," and it's become the in-thing to say. Once the trend gets started, it spreads quickly, making it hard to stop.

When my husband and I first met and he asked me on a date, I can promise you he did it with a pickup.

A Ranch Wife's Resume

Writing a good resume for a job should emphasize a person's worth. Clever wording and knowing how to highlight one's job skills, education, and experience can make a resume stand out.

Including a career objective is a good idea in order to appear motivated and goal-oriented. As an example, here's what mine would look like:

Career objective: to successfully achieve a paycheck equal to my worth or even half my worth.

It's important to include a summary of qualifications relevant to the job. Again, as an example, information I would include would be:

In good health. Rarely ill but still capable of doing most tasks when sick. Lifting capacity: upwards of half of own weight which include salt blocks, galvanized stock tanks; bags of mineral, boxes of welding rods, 40-75+ pound square bales, newborn calves, and several 24 ct. cases of beer. Adaptable to different personality types and any job environment including male-dominated, inside, outside, in good or bad weather. Energetic, enthusiastic, and outdoorsy. Ranch language and livestock terminology literate. Reading hand signals—passable.

Major strengths include:

Self-starter, self-motivated, multi-tasker, non-complainer, creative problem solver, strong-stomached, and thrifty. Versatile and self-trained to function on limited sleep; work best unsupervised. Can remain productive under scrutiny, pressure, tension, stress, and demands of upper management on short notice. Capable of running afoot from one location to another quickly; spontaneously transition from diverse responsibilities easily. Virtually maintenance free: minimal materialistic needs.

Previous jobs held and academic education information is helpful but sometimes continuing education is more impressive:

Have studied, researched, and been educated on psychology of cattle and cattle ranchers on daily basis. Have undergone training for customized ranch-related tasks to meet supervisor's expectations and satisfaction. Continue education in study of and understanding of rancher hand signal dialect.

Highlighting job skills is a must. To give you some ideas of what to include, some of my job skills would be:

Excel in usage of baling wire, duct tape, and electrical tape. Proficient in fence fixing and cooking meat-and-potatoes meals. Extensive experience in human resources: regularly use own human resources to complete light and heavy duty work. Specialize in people skills and human relations: highly accomplished in patience, tolerance, and adapting.

Knowledgeable in operating various equipment: Case IH 5250 tractor trained. Specialty trained and operate Farmall 656 Hydro and '49 Ford 8N tractors. 3, 4, 5, and 6-speed stick shifts, gooseneck stock trailers, 30' flatbed trailer, pull-type stock trailer, homemade pickup box water-hauling trailer without taillights, New Holland windrower, V and dump rakes, and other various shoddy small equipment.

Experienced purchasing agent: tractor parts and veterinarian supplies. Supplier of pantry staples, household items, bulk food for serving large crowds and specialized in purchasing beer varieties: cold, can, bottle, light, and regular.

What may be most influential is listing success stories. Mine would look like this:

Still married after 19 years. Effectively manage household and working with ranch CEO for duration of marriage. Collaborate with CEO to calve out entire cow herd; harvest hay and alfalfa crop annually. Finish tax preparation in a timely manner yearly. Co-facilitate completion of all seasonal work. Facilitate feeding crew and keeping morale positive and everyone motivated on premises 24/7/365. Single-handedly eliminated employee turnover.

Recognition and major accomplishments are also helpful. Here is what I would put down:

Periodically received appropriate credit for innovative ranch-related ideas to improve production, repair equipment, and problem-solve. Publicly recognized as a "Helluva Hand" from ranch CEO in 1998, 2005, 2011. Successfully managed to open and close a gate to stack yard (fenced-in area where our hay bales are stacked and stored) apparently designed to be opened and shut only by Army Corps. of Engineers.

As you can see, looking good on paper can help boost one's chances in advancing their career, except for ranch wives. Ranch wife resumes are nonexistent since resumes are designed to get a paying job.

Power Trip

Most guys like muscle cars, but cowboys like muscle *pickups*—four-wheel drives with diesel Cummins, Duramax, or Powerstroke engines. I just like having a little power.

It's seldom that I get to drive our souped-up pickup; a black Dodge diesel dually. The rare times I do drive it, the trailer's hooked on to haul kids to rodeos or the butcher critter for processing.

One time, my husband was forced to let me take it up without the trailer for a long-standing appointment sixty miles away, to install a power chip and get a tune-up. He had to haul 2,000 gallons of water to our cows but needed a tire on the water truck repaired first. Tackling those jobs was more than I could handle, but I had no problem handling the six-speed dually.

When he explained I'd have to take it up, like a teenager I tried to act as though it was an inconvenience and downplayed my enthusiasm for the opportunity to drive it trailer-free. And like a parent of a teenager, my husband expressed hesitancy and worry over letting me drive the dually; repeating instructions to be careful and watch out for surrounding traffic. I replied with "I GOT IT!"... "YES!"... "CAN I GO NOW?"—type responses then turned around and headed for the pickup, hiding a grin.

On the drive up while listening to the rattling diesel engine, I thought power just vibrated throughout the cab and was confident I looked impressive. It wasn't until I headed home that I understood real power, the obsession, and the reason for my limited access all this time. After hanging around for the all-day appointment I was anxious to get going. I blasted out of the parking lot saying, "WHOA!" out loud to no one in particular. A different kind of adrenaline rush came over me. I had possession of more power—power to make others envious and intimidated that a blonde chick was driving a newly enhanced heavy duty pickup. It was hard not to smile while smoking like a big black jet past sluggish cars, pickups with trailers and semis up steep hills.

I unleashed the amped-up power by persistently testing it out in various ways, I came up with reasons why I haven't been cut loose with the dually very often. I would develop an addiction to power (too late), want to trade in my SUV for a dually, get belligerent and intimidate people with the dually's size, loud rattle and monster grill, drag race other pickups up steep hills or I would get too sassy driving it (too late).

When our dog alarmed everyone I was home, my husband met me in the driveway, looking for signs of injury (to the pickup). He asked how the appointment went and sensed I was OD'd on a power trip.

I wished I would've had the power to *shut up*. I said too much about my experimental power tests and before I had a chance to come off my diesel engine high, he apprehended my power and the dually had the horse trailer back on. My husband sent me in his Dodge dually for a power *chip* not a power trip.

Why a Ranch Wife Makes a Good Friend

Having a ranch wife amongst one's circle of friends is beneficial because these women are good help and aren't high-maintenance, needy friends. Their friendship comes in handy for several reasons:

1. They carry jumper cables in their vehicle and know how to use them as well as how to check the oil and change a tire.
2. Ranch women are good cooks and have a variety of quick preparing go-to, crowd-pleasing potluck recipes they don't mind sharing. They know how and what to cook for a crowd since feeding a crew of men helping work cattle is part of a ranch wife's duties.
3. A woman who can pull, park, back up gooseneck and bumper hitch trailers, and knows how to drive a dually pickup can be of assistance in helping maneuver a vehicle in or out of tight parking spaces.
4. Any woman who lives in the country has at one time or another, dealt with exterminating varmints, rodents, and in some instances dangerous reptiles, and most likely has advice on extermination practices.
5. Ranch women are the kinds of friends who stick around when it's time to clean up after social gatherings. They've experienced both having and not having any help and know how much good help is appreciated.
6. Women who live far from town oftentimes have a pantry that's stocked better than a small town grocery store. Ranch wives are more than willing to share eggs, sugar, flour or any other staple you may be out of and urgently need.
7. If a need arises for a large roaster, stock pot, coffee urn, extra crockpot, or drink cooler, you don't have to buy one if you're friends with a ranch wife. Chances are she'll have what you need and will gladly loan it out.
8. If you have heavy or bulky items such as furniture or lumber to move, unload, or lift, a ranch wife is the ideal friend to help you because she's used to lifting heavy salt blocks, feed buckets or sacks, hay bales, stock tanks, you name it.
9. It's not uncommon for ranch women to have some experience with plumbing problems, plugged toilets, power outages, or being out of water when their husbands are gone. A ranch wife's knowledge may be helpful in solving your household dilemma.
10. If you host any kind of kitchen product party, invite a ranch wife. You can count on her attending since she enjoys an excuse to get off the ranch and is likely to make a purchase since useful kitchen equipment makes her job easier.
11. A ranch wife is a good friend to recruit on big projects that need extra help.

She won't complain about the job you assign her because she's used to being delegated, and any opportunity to work with other women for a change is welcomed.

12. Most importantly, ranch wives are sympathetic to any crisis that you encounter. They're always relieved anytime the crisis isn't theirs but are willing to help a friend out. If you're friends with a ranch wife, then you already know you've been dealt a good hand.

The Challenges of Looking Like I Have It All Together

During the winter months, in the morning, getting to appointments, church, meetings, or school sports and looking presentable are two hardships I struggle to overcome.

Our wintertime ranch chores, which have to be taken care of in the morning before we go anywhere, are the kinds of responsibilities that clash with my "good clothes." Neatly dressed women have no idea how I envy their appearance. Early morning obligations to livestock pose a challenge for farm and ranch women that most gals don't have to deal with.

Not looking like Pig Pen of the Peanuts gang in public is difficult for me when dealing with livestock. The effort it takes to keep my clothes and appearance tidy drains my energy and is the reason I am not a needy, high-maintenance kind of gal in other areas of my life. Any morning obligation that requires my appearing as well-put together as other women is expecting a lot from me. Showering, getting dressed, wrangling my hair, and shoveling down some breakfast prior to doing ranch chores oftentimes pushes me to the absolute latest it can be and still make it on time. Selecting my wardrobe usually consists of grabbing one of my old standby outfits that I'm not likely to decide to change at the last minute.

By the time I make it to my commitment, I've scrambled around pushing up hay, man-handled feed buckets to the feed bunks, refilled them, checked livestock water and hustled to get the chores done in a timely manner while my husband oversees the rest of the ranches morning responsibilities. Even though sweat may trickle down my neck during chores, I'm always hopeful that my perspiration isn't noticeable when I get to my destination.

The first thing I notice once I've finally arrived is how the people around me all seem to be more composed than I do. They have no idea that before I showed up, I was perspiring and exposed to clean clothes attractants like manure, dirt, dust, hay, livestock and livestock water.

It's usually while waiting, trying to slow down my heart rate and looking at a magazine or in my purse for something, that I observe things amiss about my appearance. I become aware that my ironed blouse has wrinkles from being squished under my coveralls or work coat. I may notice a trail of damp mud clods that lead across the office floor toward my seat. Sometimes I've spotted manure residue that clung to my shoes' soles because I made the bad decision to wear good shoes to do chores instead of changing them first.

More than once I've plucked alfalfa or hay out of my hair, but the worst is when hay has collected in my bra and I've had to nonchalantly try to remove it without other people noticing. While waiting, I've discovered dirt smudges on my pants from brushing against a muddy or dirty vehicle as I got out or recognized coffee stain dribbles on my clean pants or top. By midday I've usually found all the flaws in my appearance.

I have no problem getting it together to get ranch chores done and arriving on time, I just don't always look like I have it all together.

Hooded Sweatshirts Aren't Sissies

I couldn't survive South Dakota, winter, fall, our short-lived springs, Black Hills summer nights, or calving season without hooded sweatshirts.

I want to clarify that I don't wear "hoodies." A hooded sweatshirt is an amped up garment that is too gritty to have a sissy name. We're talking the brute of work wear.

Hooded sweatshirts go with everything no matter which job I have to do or which blue jeans I put on. They're the most versatile piece of clothing I've found anywhere. They suffice as a jacket and make a good outer layer over long underwear shirts or t-shirts. I wear hooded sweatshirts the way some people wear glasses.

My work demands durable, comfortable, non-restricting clothing especially when outside. Once I've used up the backs of my gloves to wipe my nose on, I can't use the inside of my shirt collar or hooded sweatshirt without the evidence being noticed. But more importantly, my barely-warmer-than-a-corpse body temperature demands the warmth this article of clothing can provide. These sweatshirts are a necessary staple to keep me alive in South Dakota's weather and should be our state garment.

I can't talk about hooded sweatshirts without praising the extra-large capacity, accessible front pocket. The front hand-warmer pocket makes carrying stuff handy. How many other shirts can you carry chicken eggs (*carefully*), the mail, tools, gloves, travel mugs, clothespins, candy (that you want to hide because you don't want to share), binoculars, or 4-5 cans of beer in?

The front pocket is the best place to find my car keys, ChapStick, and sunglasses. When dropped into the abyss (my purse) they disappear. A hooded sweatshirt's front pocket is where my hands hang out when they need a place to go or need to warm up or they're not busy working or flailing around helping me talk.

I normally wear the sleeves down but they adjust easily and can be pushed up when I have to get my hands dirty or cleaned up. Hooded sweatshirts with ratty-looking, stretched out elastic cuffs remain useful even if the sleeves are cut off at elbow length. These modifications allow my arms and shoulders to remain covered but eliminate sloppy stretched out sleeves that don't stay pushed out of the way when I'm trying to pull a calf, do dishes, or knead bread.

The hood can cover my head and ears in bitter cold winds but acts like a built-in scarf to keep the back of my neck warm when the hood is not over my head. The drawstrings which are designed to cinch up the hood around my face are optional accessories but I've found them to be useful for occupying my hands and helping me think better. I touch hooded sweatshirt drawstrings the way a two year-old strokes his or her blanket's satin border.

One of the hooded sweatshirt's best features is its ability to keep from unraveling. If snagged on barbwire it won't fray or get a bigger hole with every wash, and hooded sweatshirts don't necessarily need mending. It's virtually a no maintenance piece of clothing that's perfect for lazy dressers like me who avoid tops with difficult buttons, sticky zippers, or tops that need to be tucked in or ironed.

I've witnessed tourists buying hooded sweatshirts for a South Dakota memento who had no idea what they were buying. When I hear tourists call their souvenir a hoodie and talk about how comfortable their hooded sweatshirt will be for lounging around in, it's obvious they aren't aware of their souvenir's full potential. They haven't discovered the reason why such tough articles of clothing were originally called hooded "sweat" shirts.

It's Clear Where I Stand

Many times I've been told that I do a very good job at blocking a hole where cows might try to get through. I can be counted on to be standing right where they're supposed to go. I've stood in every space on Kirk ground that's known to be "in the way."

The majority of times that I've been in the way weren't my fault. I know where I'm *not* supposed to be, I just get caught standing there. Occasionally I get wrapped up in socializing with neighbors instead of paying attention to what's going on or what's coming that I often hear the second most common words my husband says to me: "GET OUT OF THE WAY!" (The first is, "I need your help for a sec.")

If Art's too far away to be heard he'll refer to his second language to get my attention—hand signals. His hand signals aren't consistent but they always mean the same thing: "You're standing in the way; get out of the way. NOW." I tend to get so focused on making sure I'm not standing where I got in trouble before—known locations where people are not to stand—that I find myself creating new "in the way" spots.

Depending on the work we're doing with our cows, I will position myself where I can still be available to re-direct errant cows if necessary, but sometimes this backfires. I've ended up being in the wrong place when an alternate route for wayward cows was being blocked with my presence.

I always know what needs done and where I need to stand, it's just that there are moments when my timing is off. In my enthusiasm to do my part, I've gotten too far ahead in the "plan" and have been known to show up at the wrong time. That's why it's never a good idea to leave my post for a bathroom break. More than once I've come around a corner of a building, pickup, or trailer and found myself in the way.

Cows always want to go in the opposite direction of where someone is standing. I tend to seek out safe places to stand that are hidden from the cows' view such as the loading chute so that I'm not blocking the cows' exit route. These have turned out to be perfect spots to be in the way also, as I found out one time when we were working cattle. My job was working in the kitchen that day preparing the meal to feed our crew, but I brought up coffee and rolls and my camera and hid in the loading chute to take pictures of our bulls being worked. Unaware of my hubby's plans for the bulls, they were turned into a holding pen leading to the loading chute instead of being let out the usual way. While snapping away with my camera, my inconvenient location was made known as my husband started bringing the bulls into my hiding spot.

Art and I have problems communicating except when we're bringing in or handling cows. I never have to worry where I stand because he makes sure I know that I'm in the way.

Getting the gate to the stackyard for Art to pick up a bale to feed our cows.
(*Photo by Art Kirk*)

Go Gaters

One of the main reasons ranchers get married is so they have a life-long companion who will always be around to open gates. This job can be very time and energy consuming for one man, so it's usually handled by his wife.

Unless we're talking King Ranch kind of wealthy, the majority of a ranch's gates are manual. When a woman is being courted by a rancher, it would behoove her to go for a drive with him to check cows to find out just what kind of rancher she's dating. If his outfit is equipped mostly with autogates or easy open-and-close gates, she can be sure he's courting her for love and not for gate reasons, but any woman who accepts a man with flawed gates is a tolerant woman and is considered a keeper by rancher standards.

These ranch closures are designed and built by men but a good share of the opening and closing of them is done by their wives. Tight, difficult-to-open and shut gates may not be a challenge for men, but getting gates of this nature can test a woman's emotional self-control and character at times. Many a gate has left a ranch woman frustrated, filled with cuss words, and even on the verge of tears, or all of the above, especially when attempting alone.

Veteran ranch wives develop or learn to use gate-opening techniques. All farm and ranch wives should take full advantage of such tricks in addition to insisting that easy gate-latching systems be installed if they are is expected to open and close gates till death do they part. It's also a good idea for wives to help each other out and exchange their gate-opening tricks.

If a ranch woman is not feeling particularly motivated to get a gate, it's important that she reassures herself that every time she has to get out, walk over to, wrestle open, drag out of the way, drag back in place, wrestle shut and walk back to the pickup, she's burning calories. Gate-getting exercise and resistance training greatly reduces the onset of arm flab and benefits one's exercise regimen while working.

Every rancher has gate-opening and closing etiquette and these men should be humored. In an industry where weather, markets, and wives are beyond a man's control, ranchers seek to maintain some sense of control in other ways. This can be in the form of systems and routines for doing things.

Gate etiquette may include the direction in which the gate should be dragged. My husband prefers gates be opened outward towards the pickup unless otherwise instructed. It truthfully does not make any difference since ranch wives are the ones getting the gates but these little micromanaging opportunities are very calming and satisfying to many ranchers.

Another gate-getting particular is standing the gate sticks vertically so there is no visible gate-sagging or leaning going on. Also, the top wire loop that goes over the gate post should rest under the nailed-in staple which suffices as a safety measure to ensure the wire loop does not get rubbed or slipped off accidentally. Of equal concern is ensuring none of the gate's barbed wires are tangled or twisted. All wires should appear horizontally straight and uniform with the rest of the fence wires. Above all is making sure the gate gets shut securely because there will be no one else to blame.

Attending to gate-getting details and being able to humor rancher fussiness are what gives ranch women a reputation for being go gaters.

Art getting a head count as our cows go through the gate headed for summer range. (*Photo by Amy Kirk*)

Ranchers

I am convinced all ranchers share the same DNA. In numerous conversations I've had over the years with my ranch-wife girlfriends and other ranch wives both older and younger than myself, I've discovered that our men have many of the same character traits because they all seem to think, react, and problem-solve in much the same way. It's also been reassuring to know that I am not the only ranch wife who doesn't understand what the heck her husband's hand signals are supposed to mean.

One of the biggest and most important roles ranchers play is being the best land stewards and conservationists of our nation. Of utmost importance to ranchers are their land and what their land provides because they are completely dependent on it. In order to continue their livelihood, they have to take care of their land. Therefore, ranchers take stewardship very seriously. If they are not good land stewards, they risk losing their livelihood. In order for ranchers to survive four and five generations, they have to be and they take great pride in that.

The other important role of a rancher is being a good caretaker of his livestock. I'm always amazed at how ranchers can take better care of their livestock than they do their own bodies. Most ranchers are obsessive about their animals' health, diet, and welfare but don't even acknowledge what their own body needs. These men think about their livestock 24/7, 365 days a year.

Ranchers are part engineer, part mechanic and part un-credited inventors.
They make do with what they have by re-using baling wire, baling twine, scrap iron,
and parts that are lying around and figure out solutions to problems that arise on the
ranch. Out of urgency and distance from the nearest parts store, ranchers are quick
to find alternative ways to solve problems. Ranch men are masters at adapting to
inconveniences, doing without, and tinkering on a problem until something works
or at least works enough to get by, but oftentimes their temporary solutions become a
permanent fix. They can think on their feet because most times they don't have a choice
especially if they're working with livestock.

They're notorious for using their tools, equipment, and tractors to do things that
their machines and equipment weren't intended for. Doing so makes for some interesting
ways of getting ranch work done such as a tractor loader sufficing as scaffolding to reach
a barn's roof for repair, but such behavior also makes great stories.

These men have also been "going-green" long before it became a trend. For
generations, ranchers have used what they have available in order to keep a ranch
running in tip-top shape. They're upcyclers, recyclers, re-users, make-doers, and get-byers.
They do things in an unconventional ways, like the old-fashioned way.

No Shirt Left Behind

I tease my husband that he wouldn't give me the shirt off his back—he
knows I'd try to get rid of it. He suffers from separation anxieties with his shirts.

I used to get after him to do something with the shirts he never wore that
weren't his style or even *in* style anymore and griped about him not wearing them.
He still has western shirts from the past three decades of every season and some
of the shirts that he wore when we were dating are prime candidates for rags. A
handful of his shirts were gifts that I've never seen him wear.

I'm mostly after the unworn, brand-new shirts with wild prints and colors
that hurt my eyes to look at and went out of style along with line dancing.. Art and
I were never the line-dancer types, and he's not a fancy shirt kind of guy—more of a
Wrangler denim snap shirts guy.

I tried getting rid of all the ones I'd never seen him wear once, but he saw
the box I had with his shirts all priced for an upcoming rummage sale. The way he
exploded at my prices could've blown a pressure cooker lid off. I argued that there
was no point in keeping them since he wouldn't wear them and I was tired of his
unworn shirts taking up all of the clothes hangers and closet space. He fumed, "But
those are fifty dollar shirts! I'm not gonna let you sell my shirts for nothin' at some
yard sale!"

If you've ever heard an annoying squirrel chattering nonstop, that's what
I sounded like as I argued my point with him that they weren't even his style and
some were so outdated they were hardly worth fifty cents. Since I'm a woman who

never forgets the past, I also reminded him how he complained about them. He insisted that I put them back, and he resolved to start wearing them for ranch work, which he did for about two months to appease me before he gradually started wearing his old favorites again instead.

Discovering how sensitive he was about parting with his unworn "fifty-dollar shirts," I was gun-shy thinking I could get rid of them without him noticing, so I boxed some up and put them in storage to see if he realized that they were missing. He'd forgotten about them for about six months, but I had to go dig them out again when he asked me what I did with them. When that idea failed, I tried forcing him to wear all the ones I wanted to throw out by boxing up his favorite Wrangler snap shirts instead. I ended up caving in though when all he had to pick from for funerals, weddings, and dates were the obnoxious-looking shirts.

Since I seemed to be the only one bugged by his loud, unworn shirts that weren't his style and was afraid of getting in trouble for purging his shirts, I compromised. I gathered up all the ones I wanted to get rid of and took them to the shop where his dirty coveralls and coats hang so he could keep the shirts he thought were still good. We were both happier because his closet space had room and hangers available, and he didn't lose his shirt on the deal.

Hammer Mechanics

Mechanics go by various titles such as repairman, Mr. Fixit, Jack-of-all-trades, or technician, but few are hammer mechanics.

The most important tool in a hammer mechanic's toolbox, obviously, is her or his temper. When a fiery temper is prevalent, progress, among other things, really takes shape—hopefully back to its former shape and not a new one.

This type of repairing is not well-known because most hammer mechanics prefer to work alone. It's a mechanical repairing art form unseen by most people because watching hammer mechanics at work can be disturbing and dangerous to some bystanders—especially spectators who habitually stare at people who get mad over their mechanical dilemmas. There's too much room for misinterpretation of a hammer mechanic's intentions, temper, or monologues.

It's not an easy mechanicing style to master. Results can vary widely depending on a mechanic's temper and skill level. The challenge lies in restoring machinery close to its original state without creating further damage, whereas traditional repairing practices rely on replacement parts, appropriate tools and money.

To learn this kind of mechanical style, brute strength and a temper are imperative. Such character traits provide the kind of motivation that gets results in the most one-of-a-kind ways. Also needed is a good, solid, hard metal object—with or without a handle—to aid in the manipulation process whether the goal is to bend metal back into its semi-original shape and intended position or to beat certain mechanical components into submission in order to get the machine or mechanism working again. Next—and most importantly—an accurate aim is needed to make substantial progress in a timely manner. The key is in having a good aim, swing, and follow-through using the right amount of forcefulness of the metal object used for manipulation.

It should be noted that important equipment shouldn't be worked on by novice, part-time, or inexperienced hammer mechanics and that this type of mechanical work is not recommended on substances that cannot withstand intense repeated pressure and forceful blows especially if aim is not consistently accurate. I speak from experience when I say miss-aim by part-timers, the inexperienced, and novices using heavy blunt objects may break non-metal substances and can further distort the shape of softer metal parts such as the aluminum running boards I hit on a gate post and failed to beat back into shape. I've had better success applying hammer mechanic techniques to other situations like loosening a gooseneck trailer's tight, semi-rusted ball-hitch collar and its rust-encrusted spring-loaded pin.

Hammer mechanical repairing techniques are not suited to just anyone either. It's especially designed for people who are impatient by nature. It takes an impatient person, lots of practice at aiming, and direct hits in order to avoid making a problem worse or creating new ones.

Hammer mechanical repairing is not recommended for the meek or mild-mannered, weaklings, or people who are calm or docile. It's more suited for people whose personalities are aggressive, enthusiastic, and blunt. Good hammer mechanics are assertive, self-motivated, strong, and deaf; or at least hard of hearing. The sign of a professional hammer mechanic at work is someone whose work echoes loudly enough through closed shop doors to be heard from across the yard.

A good hammer mechanic can work efficiently with fast turnaround time so production isn't shut down for long. Additional benefits are that there's no waiting around on someone else to work on much needed equipment.

Regardless of what the mechanical problem is, one way or another hammer mechanics get things straightened out.

Will Shop For Ads

Since the majority of women do their shopping in stores, they don't think that men enjoy shopping, but I have yet to meet a man who isn't crazy about browsing up and down the classifieds.

Men love a good classified section the way women patronize a particular grocery, department, or craft store. The classifieds are the one section of a newspaper I rarely pay attention to, but guys like my husband find them irresistible.

Classified advertisements cater to man's thinking because ads list the facts in as few words as possible, and they aren't embellished with the extra details that women are drawn to. Flyers with colorful pictures of sale items and big numbers like 30, 50 or 75 with percent symbols attached are the sales hooks that tend to snag women.

"Can you buy me a Red Bull? (energy drink) It'll give me energy for shopping."
~Myles age 10

Men also turn to the classifieds to gain new information and exchange what they've learned from the ads with each other. They recall this knowledge later, amongst neighbors, friends or relatives to start or enhance conversations or use it to dig up more knowledge about a topic related to an ad seen in the classifieds. The information that guys remember and gain from what they read in the classifieds amazes me but not as much as how many different guys see the same ads. They regularly talk about prices of hay, equipment, or property listings in ads and local guys are all aware of area auctions: whose land it is and how much land is listed. They all know what the going rate is on hay, horses, cattle, used equipment, vehicles or trailers. They pay particular attention to good deals which make for hot discussions.

"Can you pick your nose in here." (store)
~Reneé age 4

I've observed my husband as well as other men, studying the classifieds with determination as if they were studying to take the ACT (American College Testing) test. If my husband's not researching the entire classifieds section, he's tearing off a square with an ad, scratching information down on the back of a chew can or in his record book and sporting a studious look like he's memorizing key details for retrieving later. There's rarely been a family or community function where I didn't overhear men having one or more discussions over some ad listed in a daily, weekly or ag-related newspaper.

Men also enjoy browsing through people's goods listed for auction because it can be done without someone trying to persuade, pressure, or disrupt their frequent deep-in-thought decision-making moments. A guy can study or shop and compare the merchandise as long as he wants, return to it as often as he wants, and he doesn't have to wait in line if he decides he's ready to buy.

A majority of men find newspaper ads a convenient way to shop right from their recliners. Classified advertisements also allow for mulling over a prospective purchase and provide adequate time to come up with justifications for buying if there's a good deal on a trailer, tractor, baler, or other machinery that a man might not necessarily need but could use as a backup or upgrade equipment with. Men dream up uses for desired equipment the way some women create reasons to buy new cookware, kitchen appliances, or another pair of shoes.

Reading classifieds also entertains men and reduces their shopping-with-the-wife stress. Making stops for a man's wife to do her shopping can be a torturous way for a husband to spend his time unless he has some classifieds to read. For lack of a better place to be in these situations, men want ads.

Christmas Gift Ideas for Cowboys and Ranchers

When it's time to start Christmas shopping, I want to assist those people who need to give a gift to an ag man. People who have cowboys or ranchers on their Christmas lists need some good gift ideas. Many of these suggestions apply to farmers as well. With my help maybe shoppers won't resort to buying that cowboy or rancher another western shirt.

Reneé : "What does it mean when it says, 'to Art from NG'?" Amy: "Norwegian Goddess." Reneé : "Oh. I thought it meant Nag Girl."

~Reneé age 10

Starting with ranchers' interests, what comes to mind is good quality fencing equipment. Running a livestock operation requires miles of fence fixing and cobbling. Sometimes new fence has to be built or old fence has to be replaced. Consider giving good fencing pliers or quality fence stretchers—especially if you like the recipient's wife. Ranchers will pinch along with broken, rusty, hard-to-operate tools, and their wives deserve to work with better equipment. After getting frustrated with shoddy fencing equipment, I gave my rancher each of these gifts. Every time I have to fix fence I'm grateful that I gave him quality fencing pliers that open and close and fence stretchers that hold wire. Bonus tip: top the package with extra springs instead of a bow.

Depending on one's budget, electricity is a safe and useful gift. The majority of these guys believe that they can save money on electrical work for lighting in a building simply by doing the work themselves using heavy duty power cords in place of having proper wiring done, or reusing electrical wire from the 1930's. If hiring an electrician is not feasible, a free-standing shop light is a great alternative. Flood lights can be a big improvement in a shop with bad lighting as a result of a "did-it-himself" wiring job.

Since tractor-owning men are not likely to buy an owner's manual if their used farm machinery didn't come with one when they bought it, giving an owner's manual as a gift could be a time, money, sanity, and marriage saver when the equipment owner/operator has a meltdown over breakdowns. It could also greatly benefit the people who have to live with him.

For the ag man who has accumulated everything, a box of brand new nails is another superb timesaving gift idea. Depression-era raised ranchers especially, will spend hours straightening bent nails they've saved to avoid having to buy new ones.

A liniment kit for aches, pains, sore muscles, headaches, and head colds would make any cowboy, rancher or farmer feel good. These men will keep going in spite of their ailments, so why not keep them going pain free if they won't listen to sound medical advice?

A box of brand new disposable syringe needles (for livestock) would also get used…sparingly. Livestock owners and caretakers are notorious for using disposable needles beyond their recommended use in order to save money, and an entire box would last them a long, long time; or how about a new vaccine gun? A new one would be handy to have—in most ranchers' case—as a backup or as an extra and new replacement parts would extend the life of a current one that's been leaking for ten years.

For an inexpensive but long-lasting gift, consider a package of good quality, plain, black ink ballpoint click pens. If the recipient uses only one pen all the time, a whole package would last him a lifetime.

A carpentry tool kit is an ideal gift also. Unlike a chainsaw, the tools sold in tool kits were designed for construction work and do a far better job at cutting lumber accurately for constructing pole barns, calving sheds, corrals, loading chutes, and other ranch projects.

As you can see, there are plenty of things a cowboy or rancher could use. Another western shirt just isn't one of them.

Cowboy, Rancher, and Farmer Christmas Gift Guide Part II

I have a couple of decades worth of experience in agonizing over what to get a cowboy/rancher for Christmas and consider myself a seasoned gift-giver to the cowman. The extent of my husband's farming may only be putting up hay, but farmers are likely to appreciate the following suggestions also.

A milk replacer kit that includes a sturdy bucket, whisk, funnel, feeding bag and tube, and powdered electrolytes or colostrum packets would be something any farm or ranch wife would appreciate you giving her husband. It would keep him from using her good whisk and mixing bowl, and making a mess for one bottle of milk replacer when she isn't around to make it.

A good network with the right connections is important in an ag man's world. Heavy duty extension cords (to cover all electrical recommendations), power strip cords, and surge protectors are always needed since some extension cords become permanent electrical fixtures and a network of good connections is needed in the winter to plug in tractors, pickups, stock tank heaters, and tank floats.

Those ag men who bother to shave during the winter months would benefit from a hot lather machine, and their wives would get some good out of it too. It heats up a can of shaving cream, and when the cream is applied to the skin, shaving is still a chore but the heated shaving cream warms the skin first. I love borrowing the shaving cream warmer I gave my husband so much that in the winter my desire to shave my legs has increased by 5.4%.

You can illuminate any cowman's life with a good spotlight to check cows with at night during calving season. Don't sweat over trying to decide whether to get a rechargeable or a plug-in vehicle cigarette lighter type because either one will get used. If needed, the plug-in kind can easily be adapted with a little wire cutting and cobbling for use with an ATV. What's most important is that it shines a beam of daylight in the dark from a long distance.

For an inexpensive gift idea, good quality hankies or bandanas are a cowboy/rancher/farmer staple. A hanky gets left in every pickup and coat pocket and suffices as a rag or napkin in a pinch. Unlike disposable "tissues," hankies and bandanas can take getting the snot blown into them repeatedly.

The next best thing to cowmen talking about their work is watching movies that pertain to their work. Movies like the lengthy but classic *Lonesome Dove* or John Wayne classics such as *John Wayne and the Cowboys*, *Chisum*, and *Red River*, among numerous others are gifts that might inspire the cowman on your Christmas list to relax for a few hours.

It hasn't been determined if habitual temperature reading is a disorder or just part of every ag man's DNA, but the advancement of digital thermometers that record the low and the high make a worthwhile gift for the temperature-reading obsessed. It allows these men to find out what the low or high was with accuracy so they can compare this vital information at coffee or with the neighbors.

Steel posts may not seem like much of a Christmas present, but with their price having gone up considerably, new and even used ones would be received as a highly prized gift that would most definitely get used.

It should be noted that the more useless and limited a gift's abilities to produce anything or serve a worthy purpose, the more likely it should be given to a woman, not a farmer, cowboy or rancher. Gifts that are durable, multipurpose, and likely to outlive these men, or last long enough for their kids to have to deal with, are perfect. Still, no matter what gift you give, your money will not be wasted.

These industrious men find a use for whatever they're given regardless of what the gift's intended purpose is.

A Rancher's Desk

A rancher's office is outside, so naturally his desk is located in his pickup. You can learn a lot about a man by the desk area that he keeps. For instance, hair covering the seats and floor is an indication that his office assistant sheds a lot.

A rancher's desk has essential office supplies needed to conduct business on a day-to-day basis. Important papers such as toilet paper are filed in the glove compartment which incidentally, is not where gloves are kept. The easy access glove box enables a rancher to find important papers quickly.

Gloves go in the side door panel pocket, dash, tucked between the seats, behind the seats, next to the four-wheel drive gear shifter or under his office chair. Unmatched gloves are usually scattered on the floorboards, but can also be found under or behind the seat. Extra gloves are necessary in case capable, able-bodied people show up who could be put to work but don't have gloves. Those who give the lame excuse of not having any gloves are quickly relieved of their complaint because a rancher can round up a pair from his office to loan them.

Stockmen do a lot of thinking and, therefore, need lots of toothpicks in their desk console. Many-a-plan, project, problem or math has been figured out while chewing on a toothpick; an act that's important to the mulling and deliberation process a rancher has with himself.

Finding pens in a rancher's desk/console that work is rare because most guys only use the pen they keep in their shirt pocket. Cast-off pens that don't write are kept for signing big fat insurance policies, ag loans, or writing out big checks.

When the need arises to do some sorting in the office/corrals, ranchers rely on a sorting stick typically kept behind the seat. Sorting sticks also make useful pointers and counters.

Hankies and grease rags are ranch office supplies that get used daily. Both are versatile in their uses and are interchangeable if necessary.

Ranch work doesn't have any use for Scotch tape but duct tape and black electrical tape have hundreds of uses, from split fiberglass sorting sticks and cowboy boot soles that came apart to stock tank pipe leaks and vinyl seat tears, these tapes get used for fixes that only a rancher could come up with. Baling wire is also a more important staple to a rancher than is an office stapler. Wire holds stuff together better, and many ranchers keep wads of baling wire under their desk chairs. And while we're on the subject of fencing materials, fencing pliers, stretchers, clips, and staples are also kept in a rancher's office for unexpected meetings with cows out where fences are in a state of emergency repair.

A set of standard mechanical tools are always at the ready even though they're never needed until they've been removed from behind the desk for some reason. That's why a Leatherman combo tool is found in many a rancher's desk. It makes a surprisingly good substitute tool that takes care of many jobs.

Also of note, just because a rancher's desk also happens to be a vehicle doesn't mean it is okay to mess with his stuff. Most ranchers don't like dashboard and seat settings tampered with. The office equipment behind the seat can shift and settle making it difficult to move the seat back to the preferred position, and console items are kept in specific disarrangement in which only the rancher can find items. Regardless, most cattlemen enjoy visitors stopping by.

Their doors are always open, especially to those who are eligible for doing physical labor, but be warned that many ranchers have office assistants who not only shed a lot, but with whom you'll have to share your seat.

Men with Pens

A pen is a terrible thing to lose. Or so it seems for guys who are particular about their writing instruments.

Most women I know—including myself, either have a handful of pens in their purses or none at all. Since I usually try to keep several pens in my purse, I normally don't notice if one's missing, and loaning one out isn't a big deal. When all of mine are missing, my husband lends me his, but he doesn't like to make a habit of it. He only carries one pen around, and I tend to be just as careless in putting his back as I am with all of mine.

He specifically uses pens with black ballpoint ink. I've never caught him carrying the kind with colored ink, liquid gel ink, or any other type of fancy ink. He doesn't use ones with features or accessories like rubber grip barrels or caps— just the click-shut kind. His pens also need to have slim barrels in order to fit in the specially designed pen slot of his leather checkbook cover. Once he finds a good pen, he doesn't betray it by carrying around other ones. Pens get replaced only when the ink runs out.

One of my brothers has a different approach to the writing implements he favors. He'll just buy a whole box of the one he likes. Not all guys are pen specific though. Of some of the jobs I've had in town, I've had male bosses whose only pen criteria was that black ink be used on paperwork.

As a kid, I remember thinking just my dad was fussy about his pen. He'd grumble if I asked to use it, and then hand it to me begrudgingly, and say, "I want it back when you're done with it!" Using my dad's pen was serious business.

Now that I've observed defensive behavior among men who carry pens, accommodating products and pen protecting opportunities jump out at me. Besides my husband's checkbook cover, his shirts cater to a man's pen particulars. A half inch gap in the flap of Art's front pocket holds a pen securely in place when not in use, and the businesses he frequents give him pens with all the specifications most men prefer.

I witnessed pen protection at my son's wrestling tournament one time when my girlfriend borrowed her husband's pen and absentmindedly put it in her purse. Once he realized she hadn't returned it, he said with a disgusted look, "Where's my pen!?" She smiled, dug it out, and handed it back to him. He shook his head and quickly returned the pen to his shirt pocket.

When I get impatient digging in my purse for a pen and I ask Art if I can borrow his, he hesitates, hoping I'll find one before he has to loan his out. When I do borrow his pen, it's with his supervision. He waits to see if I'll forget to give it back so he can intercept it if necessary. And if I compliment his pen's smooth writing ability, he thinks I'm going to steal it.

Women can be just as particular about a pair of blue jeans—picky about the fit, comfort level, style, pants length, or brand. Still, if her husband would like the way she looks in the jeans, any old pen will do to write the check for them.

A Reputation That Stacks Up

Our ranch takes pride in what we do. As a rancher, my husband has a reputation to uphold which of course, pertains in part to hay.

There was a time when the Kirk family's reputation was based on haystacks but with the convenience of baling equipment, that reputation is now built on the appearance of round hay bales and the bale piles that are neatly stacked in rows in our stack yards.

"My dad's crackin' hay." (stacking hay)
–Myles age 3

In years past, my father-in-law's neat haystacks were noticed by people driving by— people had to drive by them while traveling Highway 385 between Custer and Pringle, South Dakota. Sometimes tourists would stop to watch and take pictures of the Kirks' hay-stacking spectacle: my father-in-law and husband working together sweeping up and stacking hay and at times arguing with each other while they did it.

Our outfit was the last in this area to stack hay. For miles around, my father-in-law was known for his haystacks. His were things of beauty; the kind that turned the heads of men who appreciated good looking haystacks.

He took great pride in his stacks and was particular about how they were built. Like all ranchers and their work, he'd perfected a system for creating works of art with his hay stacks. He wanted to retain his reputation for good-looking haystacks, so my husband was not allowed to place a sweep load of hay on top of his dad's stacks. Once my husband was in his forties and had proven himself worthy of making good sweep loads, my husband was still not allowed to stack anything.

Once we took over the ranch operation, Art was in charge of all the haying decisions. He carried on the family tradition of stacking hay for a few years, but eventually he switched to round baling the bulk of our hay crop for time-saving and convenience purposes. A good reputation for putting up nice-looking bales and having good-looking stacks of round bales begins with equipment. This gave my husband an alibi for getting a good round baler since the appearance of a guy's bales are determined by the quality of the baler that he uses.

Just because we switched to baling hay instead of stacking it, things haven't changed around here as far as putting up nice looking hay goes. I've never been allowed to run the baler, even after I turned forty, my husband only lets me windrow and rake.

There are different theories on how to stack round bales in order to shed moisture, and my rancher notices how other guys do it. The different techniques are sometimes disputed, and I can't argue with any of them. I'm not allowed to do any of the bale stacking either. Art has a system for stacking bales so they look neat and orderly from a distance.

Not only is the appearance of bales and how they're stacked at risk for criticism, the quality of a man's hay and the stack yard he puts his hay in has the potential of being judged as well. A good stack yard keeps cows out and when they're filled with neat rows of bales, the setup is noticed and admired by other hay makers. A man's reputation is at stake if any of his bales are dusty or moldy or have weeds.

Our hay really only needs to be in good standing with our cows, and so far it's always looked good enough to them to eat. The people who have seen our hay have never tried it.

All He Wants for Christmas is a New Calf Record Book

My husband looks forward to getting the same thing every year for Christmas: a new calf record book/pocket calendar. He gets anxious until he's able to transfer his important information into it before the New Year starts.

A number of years ago I started keeping a pocket calendar to write down information about our daily ranch activities that I thought I might need to reference later. My husband would ask me questions weeks, months, or even a year after we did something, like how much alfalfa seed we bought the year before, what we paid for it, if I remembered what day it was that we doctored a certain calf, bought a bull, or sold open cows (not bred or lost a calf before or after its birth), and I'd have to find out for him. Looking it up in my pocket calendar was quicker than digging through a drawer full of files for a particular invoice or retracing days and months in my head.

Several times I had mentioned to him that he should start writing stuff down in a book of days so he wouldn't have to always ask me, but I worded my suggestion wrong. He assured me he wasn't a writer and wasn't going to keep a "diary." He'd seen how much I filled up each day's little square of my pocket calendar, to him the equivalent of a girl's diary. The only recording he did was jotting down calving dates and calf details in a thin, pocket-sized calf record book.

One December, his mom sent him the complimentary pocket-sized calf record book with weekly calendar her vet gave her, thinking he could get some use out of it. At first Art stashed it in the junk drawer because he was used to the thinner, plain old calf record books that he used every year.

About the same time his mom sent the record book, my mom told him about a farm couple she knew who kept a daily log of their farm and ranch activities. Keeping track of all kinds of farm and cattle-related information on their operation in a book had come in handy for them, especially at tax time.

When our son Myles was about eight and calving season was starting, he wanted his own calf record book to record cows' calving dates and the details of their calves just as his dad did. Art went to the junk drawer and dug out the red calf record book/pocket calendar to give Myles. Art was rummy from lack of sleep and struggling to remember what day it was, what he'd done the past few days, and what information needed to go into our son's calf record book. While thumbing through the red calf record book/calendar before giving it to Myles, Art had a revelation. I left the room, and when I came back he was at the kitchen table writing stuff down in the red one his mom sent him and our son was packing around his dad's thin, basic calf record book.

The next time my mom visited, she noticed my husband jotting stuff down in the record book/pocket calendar. He told her how her advice was one of the best suggestions he ever got in helping him keep track and remember stuff. Of course that really made me mad because I didn't get the credit for mentioning the exact same thing numerous times before my mom ever made the suggestion. So now, if I want him to take my advice sooner, I just tell our mothers.

My Retirement Fund

Some women have an addiction to shoes. Their closets overflow with a wide variety of shoe colors, heel heights, and seasonal trends in footwear. No matter how many pairs they own, they're always on the lookout for another pair. Oftentimes their men don't understand or appreciate their wives' shoe craze.

I can relate to a man's annoyance with his wife's personal shoe shop. My husband has a fetish for hats. A summer straw cowboy hat, a felt cowboy hat, and two ball caps—one for work and one for special occasions—are not enough to satisfy him. Most of my husband's hats are collected in three stacks on top of the gun cabinet: straws, felts, and caps, but hats exist in other rooms as well.

Some of the cowboy hats are black felt, others are silverbelly and he has a couple of brown felt cowboy hats from his childhood. His summer collection consists of four varieties of straws. I've never taken time to count the scotch caps, and we haven't even covered the stack of ball caps yet.

Felt cowboy hats are spendier and take longer to break in, so I guess I should be thankful he draws the line somewhere. It just seems ridiculous to me that once winter is over he and our son are soon wearing different straw hats from the new "spring collection."

> *"This is my good luck hat so I don't die." (cowboy hat while riding)*
> *‒Myles age 12*

Regarding the stack of caps, Art has the freebee hats from auto and tractor dealerships, gift caps from friends or relatives, hunting season caps, and bought-on-a-whim caps. I had no idea how particular he is either. He prefers a certain style to the caps he wears. If he gets a cap that doesn't fit his criteria, it doesn't get ditched or given away; it gets stacked instead.

I have yet to see him get rid of any caps voluntarily. I've suggested wearing them for dirty work in the shop and threatened to decorate with them or create gag gifts from them, but my suggestions are fighting words. He's possessive of his collection and his tight-hide nature won't allow him to give or throw any of them away, unless he gives it to Myles. He knows their worth or what he paid, thus an investment's been made. If I try getting rid of them behind his back, he notices and we argue over why he bothers to keep them. When I get tired of looking at the "stacks" and my frustration is maxed, I sort off the ones he doesn't wear and haul them to the shop work bench. This way I'm not accused of getting rid of them and I don't have to look at them. Eventually, they'll hang from the rafters of the shop.

> *"It's like a dog's [territory]—I don't want someone else's scent on it." (his favorite hat)*
> *‒Myles age 12*

Cowboy hats on the other hand, don't hang from the shop rafter nails that easily, so until I find a solution I get to watch the cowboy hat stack grow. Our poor son got sucked into this hat hoarding habit from a young age. By the time Myles was ten he had fourteen caps, four straws, and three felt cowboy hats.

One day their hat collection will be considered "vintage." Then they'll really be worth something. Art and I can retire off the sale of his hat collection from the auction I plan to have someday of the hat stacks.

Cowboy MacGyver

If you've ever watched the hit TV show *MacGyver* from the 80's, then you have a good idea of what my husband is like—a handsome, intelligent, and clever guy.

Not only does my spouse possess good looks and charm as MacGyver does, but Art's also ingenious in getting out of a bind with ordinary objects lying around. He uses everyday stuff to come up with a plan no matter what kind of situation he stumbles into.

Besides their footwear, clothes, and hairstyles, the only other difference between MacGyver and my spouse is how they react under pressure. MacGyver may be calm, collected and even-tempered but interestingly, it was my husband's MacGyver-like skills combined with his spirited emotions that contributed to successfully getting us home when we had car trouble once.

While we were headed out for a date night in falling snow that was getting increasingly treacherous, our car's weakening alternator caused the headlights to dim drastically and reduce our visibility to five feet. In the deserted parking lot of a restaurant in the tiny town of Rockerville, South Dakota, my hero restored the headlights to their full brightness with help from his frustration and a tire iron. He banged on the stuck alternator brushes and miraculously, the headlights brightened up. His trick allowed us to see in order to turn around and get back home.

When our pickup's heater control knob broke off, he used a pair of pliers and an empty brass bullet casing rolling around on the floorboards to replace the knob. His ingenuity enabled us to resume arguing over where the heater knob should be set.

In the television show, MacGyver is never without his Swiss Army knife. Similarly, Art always has a wad of baling wire handy. This wire has aided our ranching operation in numerous predicaments, but it also held my old car's headlight and battery in place for several years before I got a different vehicle.

A good grease rag has proven invaluable as well. They can replace a missing cap or lid, plug a hole, tie things up, wrap greasy parts in, or blow one's nose into. Other items that have helped my husband improvise his way out of dilemmas have included good old reliable duct tape and black electrical tape.

It was trusty duct tape that sufficed as the driveline couplings in place of the real ones that were unavailable at the time of the manual transmission installation of a father-son ranch pickup project (now parked at our junk yard). Duct tape and tire patch adhesive also repaired our daughter's bicycle tire tube.

When a pickup tire got a hole in it, he remembered being told once that adding antifreeze to the inside of the tire would seal the leak which it did so he didn't have to take it to town right away. Another time he used a thick rubber glove found under a pickup seat to stop a stock tank leak. My cowboy MacGyver siphoned water from an overfull stock tank into a secondary empty one using a flexible plastic pipe he found after work on the tanks had been done recently. A memorable improvisation our kids will never forget was witnessing their dad's quick thinking skills to kill a rattlesnake using a steel post he had in the pickup box.

My husband's been able to improvise his way out of predicaments with whatever was handy and has always looked good doing it, but the key item that has consistently relieved him of these kinds of stressful experiences has been Excedrin.

The Original Recyclers

I hate to deflate the enthusiasm of "going green" newbies, but our nation's ranching forefathers were the original recyclers, up-cyclers, re-users, and reducers.

People who have been far-removed from relying on the basic necessities of life and are just now realizing they can recycle things may think that the concept of the three R's (reduce, reuse, recycle) is a modern revelation. Such thinkers may be technologically fast-paced but are slow conservatively. Ranches have lived the three R's for generations.

After decades of discounting the way ranchers live, the rest of society is finally catching on and adopting ranchers' philosophy for repurposing things, conserving, and living within their means. More and more people are finding joy in discovering new ways to use their discarded stuff. Take dingy-looking, holey, threadbare underwear with a waistband that's lost its elasticity. Once it's no longer wearable, it makes a perfectly good grease rag, dust cloth, dog chew toy or in desperate situations, maybe even cheesecloth.

"I can sell my old ones to Dad." (old toy guns to get new ones)

~Myles age 6

As a result of carrying on the tradition of living frugally and resourcefully, ranch outfits have set the gold standard beyond anyone's imagination in recycling and conservation by using what they have lying around. Greenhorn recyclers can only aspire to be as resourceful as people in agriculture who have a lifetime of personal experience and a family history of repurposing and upcycling stuff. The habit of saving objects for future reuse that out-used their intended purpose is a family tradition on ranches. Just ask any rancher what's in his junk yard. A good look around any long-standing ranch will indicate how economical and resourceful ranchers are. Or what kind of junk they're partial to.

With a few tools and a strong desire to refuse to pay what the parts would cost, a rancher can part-out equipment and reincarnate it into something useful again unless it involves a motor. Then it may take a little longer before it is useful again.

With a little imagination and a welder, Art built us sturdy coat hooks for our closet from repurposing old horse shoes; wagon wheels became gates for our yard, a short-lived TV stand—I got tired of stubbing my toe on it—and a coffee table for friends. My husband also custom-made our yard fence out of old oil field drill pipe.

I have yet to see anyone else who has used hubcaps for a dog dish, a broken-handled cook pot for a feed scoop, or an old refrigerator drawer for an oil pan. Every ranch uses old tires for feed tubs, stock tanks, retaining walls or loading ramps, and no cow outfit is complete without its supply of five gallon buckets and lick tubs that can serve hundreds of other uses once emptied. Bed springs may be obsolete, but when connected together, they make a useful fence for protecting hay bale stacks from deer and elk. We've always used old window screens to scoop off algae in stock tanks and have yet to find a better mouse-proof storage unit than a discarded microwave. Even seat belting has been repurposed into strapping on an ATV rack to hold baby calves during transportation to the barn.

Ranch families have always considered their natural as well as previously purchased resources a precious commodity because most outfits aren't located near Walmart when something is needed on the ranch. Practicing conservation and the three R's is an age-old tradition with families who ranch because it coincides with being a tight-hide (thrifty) and resourceful, and has been the basis of ranches for hundreds of years when a family couldn't get to town.

I'm grateful for our recycling forefathers because without the old farm machinery perched near the turnoff to our place I wouldn't know what landmark to use to describe to visitors where we live.

Motivationally Speaking

Of the most influential motivational speakers I've heard, ranchers top my list. The general public may not categorize ranchers with such speakers but cattlemen have equally influential communication skills.

The purpose of a motivational presentation may include persuading workers that they're capable of doing challenging tasks, provoking a specific reaction, or spurring attendees into action. All motivational speakers have their own techniques for conveying a convincing message. A rancher's message sometimes includes hollering.

Many of the ranchers I know swear by the old-fashioned motivation that they grew up with. To help persuade audience members that these old-school techniques have successfully worked in the past, ranchers like to include personal experiences. My husband shares his regularly. His dad used old-fashioned methods which always motivated Art to pay attention and not make the same mistake twice.

When presenting a talk to their crews, ranchers live by the old adage that less is more. They prefer to keep explanations to a minimum using as few words as possible to effectively get a point across—preferably verbs and one-syllable words, if at all possible. Popular words or phrases to spring subordinates into action include: "MOVE!," "LIFT!," "HUSTLE!," "GET BACK!," "HURRY UP!," "HOLD 'EM!," and "GET OUT OF THE WAY!" Proper inflection and body language are equally important in rallying troops.

Additionally, persuasive facial expressions and making eye contact help to deliver a clear message but are reserved for important moments when influence is critical. If these are overused, listeners eventually ignore them and the effectiveness in communicating immediate action or key points is lost. Nonverbal communication such as a furrowed brow, clenched jaw, and dilated pupils can boost any message and propels people to try harder. Together, these techniques work to instill the kind of action that may entail lifting heavy salt blocks, empty but still heavy galvanized stock tanks, heavy square bales or filled five gallon buckets. These techniques are also used on crewpersons during critical moments when safety is at risk while working with cattle or livestock that must not escape through visible openings.

In order to avoid a situation getting out of hand on big jobs that a small crew is expected to do, it's especially important that everyone's roles and the overall plan is not misunderstood. When necessary, our ranch's motivational lecturer will speak in a dialect that provokes and rouses his staff to engage quickly if the potential for disaster is about to strike. Such instances include the potential for cows getting around a rider, slipping through a gate or a hole, a lead cow steering the herd in the wrong direction, a calf that wants to turn back, or a bunch of skittish heifers about to bolt away from the open gate right at the makeshift corral made of portable panels.

After a difficult task is finished, our family's motivational spokesperson will oftentimes refer to the reason for using old-fashioned motivational practices at work: "There's a turning point in every project that determines whether you succeed or fail." That critical moment is when workers need to be motivated, persuaded, roused, made mad or provoked into action. Old-fashioned motivation is just another way of saying, "YOU CAN DO IT!" when accomplishment seems impossible, but probably more important is when not doing it isn't an option.

An added bonus to hearing ranchers speak is that their motivational talks are affordable for everyone. The most cost-effective way to benefit from their presentations is to pay attention.

Looking at Figures

Once my family and I (with the help of our vet and neighbors) pregnancy check all of the cows and implement our fall vaccination and calf preconditioning program, we can focus on what comes next—speculating.

Mid-fall signifies a time of year I spend constantly looking for a calculator, when the end of the ranch calendar year is nearing. After sale day of our calf crop, the new ranch year begins. Until we sell our calves there's a lot of market checking, penciling-out, reviewing weekly calf sales, and predicting going on at our house. It's a flurry of numbers around here. Figures are written on the backs of chew cans, newspaper corners, calf record books, napkins, kids' homework and the like. All my husband wants from me is a calculator and his glasses.

As soon as the livestock newspapers arrive in our mailbox, the pages containing recent calf sales listed for area sale barns are reviewed followed by rigorous analyzing. The market report's pages are scanned to see who has sold already, where they sold, what their calf weights are, what their calves brought, and what the latest weigh-up prices are.

Fall is the season when my husband spends more time checking out the figures on our cows than he does on mine. After we've worked our cows, several important numbers get recorded in the calf record book. At the top of the list are the confirmed head count of how many calves are going to the sale barn, the total heifer calves, bull calves and the kids' calves—heifers and bulls. All are listed on a back page of the record book. Next is the list of opens (unbred) and lates (expected to calve late season) by their ear tag numbers; then there's the cull cows and the kids' cull cows list that will also to go to town and their ear tag numbers.

Some figures get recorded to memory instead, including the number of calves speculated to get docked for frost-bit ears, red-coloreds, rat tails, tight-hides, and any other visible character flaws that are likely to cause calves to get sorted off and sold separate from the main bunch. Other mentally noted figures are the calf weight guesses my husband and I discuss of the heavies and the lights (weights of the calves) which will be checked against the sale barn's scales on sale day. Even though they're practically memorized, the lists and ear tag numbers written down are reviewed repeatedly.

All of this tallying and speculating leads to further analyzing in other areas of concern pertaining to numbers. More calculating is done on our winter feed supply. Bales in each stack yard—grass and alfalfa—gets recounted and the numbers get checked against what the record book says. Then estimates are made on how many hay-feeding days at most we're likely to have, how many days we'd have enough hay to feed our new herd size after culling, and a rough date of how long our hay could be expected to last.

Even when our calf check is in hand, I know better than to put the calculator away. The whole ninety mile drive home from the sale barn my husband will have me calculating post-sale figures. He spends a lot of time checking numbers because he's like every other rancher. He likes to see good looking figures.

The Ultimate Meat Skeptics

For people who like to eat but who question whether or not beef is safe to eat, I would encourage them to dine with the world's biggest meat critics: ranchers. Trust me, having lunch or dinner with a rancher will eliminate all skepticism.

The only thing that's tainted about American beef is the lack of accurate information given to the public and especially the proper handling and preparing it. Preventing food-borne illnesses simply takes some precautionary measures but, most importantly, cooking the meats at the proper internal temperature: 160 degrees for hamburgers, 145 degrees for roasts and steaks. For those who don't have a meat thermometer, I'd be willing to bet their states' Beef Council would send one along with correct information answering any questions regarding what people have "heard" about beef.

Ranchers are notoriously finicky about their meat. I have firsthand experience dealing with such behavior, but my conversations with other ranch wives verify that meeting any ranchers' high expectations of meat doneness is a standard marital challenge.

Cattlemen are the ultimate connoisseurs of beef. Besides potatoes and maybe bread, beef is pretty much the basis of what they eat, and the last thing they want to do is jeopardize their dinner. Cattle-producers know their product, and ranching families rarely experience food borne illness from beef because they know how to properly prepare and cook it.

Like most ranchers, my husband likes his beef cooked to his specifications regardless where it was cooked: at home, at cookouts hosted by friends or family, in restaurants, at fast food drive-thrus or at concession stands. If there's any question, he gives it the fork lift or cuts into it for further inspection. Beef is king in our home and for good reason. We need the energy it provides to do the labor-intensive work that ranching requires. Beef is satiating, tasty, and provides necessary nutrients (zinc, iron, and protein among others) for energy.

The beef my family and I eat typically comes from younger stock we cull for noticeable imperfections or character flaws that are not likely to generate enough income at the sale barn to make it worth the trip of hauling it there. We grain feed it for flavor purposes (we prefer the flavor of grain-fed over grass fed beef) for a few months and have it processed locally, but we have also eaten beef that originated from other ranches in the United States and sold in grocery stores, retail warehouses, and butcher shops. When the freezer's meat supply is low, it makes a lot more sense to pick out a cull that will provide more for us as a year's food supply than it would as income that in all likelihood wouldn't pay the gas to get it to a sale barn.

If people need proof that American beef is safe to eat then they should read the label's expiration date, ensure it's been kept cold, wash their hands before handling, use different platters and utensils for cooked and uncooked meats, and cook the meat until it reaches the right internal temperature. Still, any skeptic's best bet is to find out what a rancher orders when he goes out to lunch or dinner. Producers believe in beef because they're the ones who work hard 365 days a year producing and raising it. Regardless of what else is on the menu, 90% of ranchers will order steak or prime rib. The other percentage will order a hamburger.

There are no stricter or more fanatical meat critics than cattlemen. Going out to dinner with them can be just as aggravating as cooking for them. Once they've eaten steak or prime rib at a restaurant that cooked it to their satisfaction and met their high expectations, they become loyal patrons. They're not interested in trying out new restaurants their wives suggest if they've found a place that serves good beef consistently cooked the way they like it, be it well-done or medium rare. Any restaurant that a rancher patronizes regularly is getting the highest compliment and seal of approval it can receive. Ranchers know the difference between quality beef cuts and cheaper beef cuts as well as what their preferred doneness should look like because they've lived on a diet of different cuts and grades of beef most of their life. They can tell when an eating establishment knows good beef and how to cook it to perfection when they get a steak cooked exactly the way they think it should be and has excellent flavor.

The best way to reassure those who question beef's quality, healthiness, and safety is to dine next to a rancher. Notice what the cattlemen are eating at a restaurant and tell the waiter, "I'll have what he's having."

Man Soap

Many wives like to set out foofy potpourri-smelling bar soap for hand washing. This makes it hard for husbands to get a handle on a bar of soap.

When floral and potpourri smelling soap lingers on a man's hands, it can be a grim reminder that his man card (masculinity) is being tugged on ever-so-slightly out of his hands. Washing hands with feminine-smelling pansy soap is not something that should be handled delicately.

For starters, men need soap that smells appealing to them; something like beer, pickups, or grilled meat would be good, but unfortunately the idea hasn't hit the market yet. For now, most men just want a bar of man soap that doesn't smell like a woman's bathroom or her scented candles. Some women are unaware that there is soap just for men. There's only one. It's gritty and removes dirt, grease, grime, and dead skin. It's called Lava soap. It even smells gritty; like sand and gravel.

Lava isn't hard to find on soap isle shelves because men don't need 43,756 soaps to choose from. A guy can only wash with one bar of soap at a time. Lava is the easiest to identify because it's the only soap that comes in a red wrapper with a dormant volcano on it, which ironically, is a good representation of my husband. Art occasionally erupts when he wants to clean up after a particularly grime-ridden day and there's no Lava soap in the soap dish. When the black grime won't come off with my nice-smelling soap he'll shout in a disgruntled tone, "WHERE'S THE LAVA?"

For those of you who have never heard of Lava soap or experienced Lava's claim to fame that it's "pumice powered," let me enlighten you. Take a piece of 220 grit sandpaper and wrap it around your favorite moisturizer bar; add a little water and apply to skin. It scrubs off embedded dirt and leaves the skin feeling sloughed but clean. There's a reason why it's called *hand* soap, ladies.

Lava is the John Wayne of soaps: tough and abrasive. The only thing that's soft about this volcanic soap is its color—it's a muted manure green shade. Lava also contains "moisturizers," which appears to be an oxymoron but is actually a selling point to target women—the ones most likely in charge of buying soap.

Man soap can do it all—including slowing down the onslaught of baldness. Like most male-targeted merchandise, men are industrious at finding many other uses for a product originally designed for one purpose. I heard about a guy who used Lava soap not only to exfoliate his head but used it to stimulate his hair follicles and promote hair growth. Who knew?

The point I'm trying to make is that men can't do these things with soap that melts into a greasy, slimy puddle when the soap has set in water too long, nor can men come clean about trying such hair-stimulating experiences if they don't have any Lava to do them with. As a family's primary caretaker and shopper, it's a wife's duty to provide the means necessary for her husband to stimulate his hair follicles if he wants to or scrub his hands clean. Wives agree to love, honor, and cherish their husband's man card by having their spouse's preferred soap available. It's pertinent that wives get a handle on this before husbands threaten to pull the woman's card: the credit one she uses when shopping, because quite frankly, and my husband will attest that, the replacement of Lava soap with scented soap has gotten out of hand.

Art wearing the same shirt he wore on our first date in 1993—now a work shirt.
(*Photo by Amy Kirk*)

Cowboy Shirts That Fit

I can still remember the shirt my husband wore on our first date like it was yesterday. That's because he *was* wearing it yesterday.

Upon close examination of the long-sleeved western shirts that hang in a cowboy's closet, one might see how ranching cowboys' (different from PRCA rodeo cowboys) loyalty to things of importance could be measured by their devotion to the shirts they wear. When they find something that works well, they intend to keep it. Take me for instance. My husband's hung onto me for so long he must have approved of my work ethic tending cattle, doing chores, cobbling fence together and handling cow-related wrecks. And he hasn't had me near as long as the shirts he's been wearing since before we were dating.

Long-sleeved western shirt advocates favor this particular style because it's a snap to wear them for any occasion. An all-season, utility-type shirt equipped with pockets that a guy can stow his chew can, record book, and pen in, these functional items of clothing also shield men from the scorching summer sun—a cowboy's alternative to greasy sunscreen—scratchy hay, barb wire, chilly breezes, and welding slag.

Ranch cowboys don't wear shirts to impress people. They wear their shirts to look proper for weddings, funerals, going out for steak dinners, or just to get work done. Style and trendiness or, for that matter, getting greasy, muddy, manurey and grass stained, isn't a concern.

Instead of wasting money frequently buying new duds, these cowboys utilize their current wardrobe the way people used to wear clothes—for the lasting durability and to get the goody out of every fiber until it looks like cheesecloth.

I can tell which decade my husband's shirts came from according to their style and brand, and some of them are approaching their silver anniversary. Just because a shirt starts to show a little age, signs of wear, or is considered ugly by a ranching cowboy's standards doesn't justify giving up on it or getting rid of it. These guys are fair and impartial to all their clothing no matter what their likeability for a particular shirt is or how they ended up with it. Each one is given a chance to do its part in a cowboy's world at one time or another.

Most cowboys don't want to detract friends and neighbors from approaching them by wearing "loud" or unsightly shirts when they go to town for an outing. To these men, sharp contrasting, bold, and brightly colored shirts or shirts with western scenes are saved for ranch work where people aren't likely to see them wearing such clothing. Disliked shirts are worn while checking cows, on fencing projects, doing chores, or to places where cowboys are likely to be alone.

Plain and simple western shirts are more apt to be worn when going out. The less complicated the patterns and colors, the more camouflaged he is for blending into the public environment. Basic western shirts allow cowboys to mix well with others. Ranching cowboys look sharp wearing expensive brand new shirts, but the ones that seem to suit them the best are like their ranch wives: unflashy, dependable, tough, and last a lifetime.

DIY Pole Barn

Ranchers like my husband know what it takes to build a stout pole barn for calving. That's why he built ours himself.

Our ranch operation managed to get through a lot of calving seasons but eventually my husband decided it was time to put the old barn out of its misery and rebuild. He cleared the area to construct a much bigger calving barn and proceeded to dig himself several holes; enough to build a 30x60 foot pole barn.

To get started, we needed a lot of electrical poles, mostly because of all the poles we had piled down at the junk yard, several were rotten inside or too crooked, not just the normal crooked he could work with. He also planned to use several poles to make a tack room and calving stalls along both walls of the barn and an alleyway big enough to park the tractor in.

By doing the construction work himself with the help of our son Myles, he estimated that his do-it-yourself barn would cost us a fraction of a company built one roughly the same size, but we all know how those deals work. DIY projects come with a price. My husband stated several times about the building throughout the barn's progress that, "It isn't goin' to the county fair," but his DIY builder's anxieties also caused him to have nightmares of the barn turning out severely crooked when finished.

Our barn is visible from a nearby road, and everyone who knows us was very interested in our building project, especially the county. After getting the electrical poles in place, the county was thoughtful enough to send us a great photo of the beginning stages of our pole barn—which was nice since I hadn't gotten around to doing it yet—along with a note saying that either we didn't have our building permit visible or we didn't file for one. We didn't get one to begin with because it wasn't on the list building needs. It was, however, a big oversight.

Neighbors who passed by our place monitored our barn building activity from the get-go, and whenever the opportunity presented itself, they generously offered their observations, comments, and suggestions. Strangers and tourists driving past our barn just gawked when they drove by. This is likely because they'd never seen anyone use a ladder with a tractor loader to reach a barn's peak; something they would have known about if they had read OSHA's latest volume of "New and Unusually Unsafe Practices."

The main objective to building a new calving barn has been to have a place to go if my husband or I are in the dog house, but having a bigger barn has also come in handy at calving time so it's been called "the calving barn." Since the new barn is more than double the size of the old one, essentially it's a place where we have twice as much work to do during calving in extremely cold weather conditions than we did before.

After observing how my husband tackled this big building project amidst all the other ranch work we had to do, I gained even more respect for him. I admired his persistence despite all of the challenges he had to overcome throughout each of the building stages, but what I admired the most about him on this project was how good he looked in an apron while hammering away.

What Really Counts

People who spend any amount of time around a rancher should expect to be asked to count something sooner or later. My rancher counts money, days, years, bales, and elk, but mostly cattle.

After selling culled cows at a sale barn, he counts each day that the expected check hasn't come in the mail. Once it arrives, he reminds me how many days have passed that I still haven't deposited it. He recounts to me how many times he's already explained his plan for the day and frequently shares with me how many years I have argued with him about the same things we've squabbled about since we got married.

If I mention seeing elk grazing in our hay fields he'll ask how many I saw, whether they were at home or up at the barn by Pringle, whether there were any bulls and how many. He usually confirms my numbers against the neighbors' within a couple of days.

He also keeps a running tally for every load of water I've hauled in order to track how much we owe the town of Pringle. When preplanning our winter feed regimen, Art counts out roughly how many days our hay bales are expected to last. A page in his record book is dedicated to how many bales we put up over the summer, and this is broken down into the number of bales we got off every hay field in addition to how many are round, square, alfalfa, and grass. He also keeps stats on all the hay that's been carried over from the previous year and a list of that hay in grass, alfalfa, round, and squares. Another page has all the number of bales put up for each year since 2003 (when he started using a record book to keep track) for comparison purposes.

Other important numbers have to do with selling our calves in the fall. Besides our calf crop, a few calves are the kids' so he distinguishes a head count of ours versus the kids'. Some calves we expect to get docked on price for flaws in appearance or other problems and he estimates a head count of those. A head count and an estimate on what the calves weigh determines how many cattle pots we need for shipping our calves to the sale barn. After the sale, he has a new set of numbers for figuring out what the average amount per head came out to be.

Habitual counting stems from the all-important head-counting of cattle. Bulls, culls, cows, pairs, heifers, drys (not lactating) and opens (not bred) are counted throughout the year. Getting a head count is done from the inside or the outside of a fence, along the highway, or if the neighbor's cattle end up with ours by accident or vice versa. Counting as cows go through a gate is most popular, but they also get tallied before, during, and after sorting, while moving to a new location, or once they've all arrived at a water source.

I don't like counting because I always come up with different numbers every time I count cattle. They don't stand still or go through gates one at a time very well and are hard to differentiate when they're close together and all look the same—black.

Over the years, I've learned that just getting a number is what really counts. If my husband asks me what I got for a head count, saying, "I didn't count," is the wrong answer.

'Tis the Season to be Hairy

Biting wind and freezing temperatures forewarn me it's going to happen, but when my husband decides to grow a beard, it takes me a while to warm up to the idea. I'm often resistant to the changes of his facial hair until it reaches my husband's goal—a mustache.

By the time I get used to the feel of his face at a new beard-growing phase, I have to get used to his whiskers all over again when they grow to another new phase. The first stage of his beard growth is coarse and sandpapery. Initially, I tell myself the upside to this rough stage is that I can skip exfoliating my face in the morning because my husband will do it for me every time he gives me a smooch. That is until it feels like a rash has developed on my beard-sensitive face. Within a week though, his facial hair outgrows that stage and his whiskers become more like a prickly cactus swiping my chin and cheeks instead.

By stage three, his beard hair has gotten longer but still doesn't lie down, so the whiskers on his upper lip collide with my nose when I try to start the day out with a quick kiss from him. I'm more accepting of my husband's winter beard idea once his facial hair reaches what I call the "teddy bear face" stage, when his whiskers have grown out enough that it doesn't scratch like a wire brush and scour my face raw anymore.

Beards aren't my husband's facial hairstyle preference, but rather a means towards achieving big mustache status that resembles actor Sam Elliott's mustache. Art's not fond of the clean-shaven appearance except for emerging mustache whiskers, so he grows out a full beard first. Once his mustache whiskers reach a desired length, the rest of the beard comes off.

I appreciate that he makes an effort to keep his facial hair looking clean and orderly, except when he and I are vying for use of the bathroom mirror when we're getting ready to go someplace. Besides getting reacquainted with my husband and his whiskers, I have to brush up on my sharing skills with the mirror in the cramped quarters of our only bathroom.

It wasn't spoken in our wedding vows, but I've since learned that part of my promise to a man who occasionally grows facial hair is that I'm committed to letting him know if his beard or mustache needs attention. It takes me a while to get into the habit of remembering to mention these details the first few months of being around my husband with a beard or mustache. I act as a stand-in mirror for him if real mirrors aren't available by having to verify if his mustache looks alright. It's my duty as his trusted wife to warn him if his facial hair is amiss or needs a napkin swipe.

The one thing that I have gotten used to is once he's made up his mind about something, he doesn't change his decision, and I just have to face it. More than pokey whiskers, any attempts I make to persuade him to do otherwise just get in the way.

More Reasons to Thank America's Farmers and Ranchers

When our country needs its citizens to do their patriotic duty, farmers and ranchers can always be counted on. They regularly stimulate the U.S. economy with their generous contributions in equipment repairs and help secure the employment of mechanics and the employees in the equipment parts department across America.

Tractor and implement parts and repairs can get pricey. The standard for charging seems to be the more the machinery is urgently needed, the bigger the repair expense seems to be. The business of fixing or replacing parts in farm and ranch equipment is similar to the funeral business. It'll never die. If it wasn't for equipment that's depended on, used, and breaks down on a regular basis, there wouldn't be expensive parts, extensive repairs, or extreme rebuilding to pay for in order to keep equipment going another 16,034 hours (if the hour meter even works). Today's farm and ranch machinery is expected to run fairly steady in order to keep up with the ever growing demand to produce high quality nourishing food to feed the world—whether the product is grown specifically for human consumption or livestock consumption.

Unfortunately, tractor and implement parts aren't standard or readily available on Walmart shelves. What's considered a substantial amount of money to an ag man is spent on parts and labor to restore equipment back to operating status. As long as people and animals need food, tractors and their implements will keep the parts-men and mechanics employed. Such highly depended upon equipment is all part of enabling farmers and cattle producers to keep up with the increasing world population's appetite for food.

In addition to spending a lot of their money to keep their equipment working, men in agriculture also spend a small fortune on pop and candy bars—the workin' man's quick-fix sustenance of choice. Such purchases may seem meager but they add up for the economy's sake. Not only are they a convenient, easy-to-eat-on-the-fly kind of food and quick energy-boosters, they further contribute to the fight against hunger by allowing other people to eat the healthier foods farmers and ranchers produce. Pop and candy bars stave off guys' hunger a little longer, keeping these men awake and allowing their tractors to continue doing farm work, putting up hay, storing feed, etc., but more importantly, guys don't have to waste time stopping to eat lunch when a lot of work needs to get done.

Modern tractors are equipped with computers that rely on other computers' expertise to find the problems and call for certified or specially trained mechanics to fix them. In today's technological world, instead of putting the farmers' and ranchers' industrious nature to good use repairing their own equipment, they're having to put it to use finding new ways to continue producing food for the world using fewer natural resources and in spite of the various vice-grip-like restrictions that are currently putting the squeeze on their livelihood. They may only account for 2% of the U.S. population but they still manage to crank out food that feeds people all over the planet.

Farmers and ranchers don't like to have their equipment break down, to wait for parts to come in or repairs to get done, to spend money to get their expensive machinery fixed, or to hold up work that needs to get finished up, but they can enjoy eating a hot lunch.

Trade Skills

My husband's vehicle trading skills are more attractive than the pickups that we trade-in. When we decide it's time to upgrade a ranch pickup, he uses clever strategies to "trade off" our trade-ins.

We try to get every penny's worth and more out of our pickups by using them long after they've been depreciated out. As a result, our pickups are far from eye-appealing to an average used-pickup buyer. A pickup's appearance doesn't do it for either of us because we're more interested in its ability to do as many different jobs as possible. So long as it still runs and the vitals work—like the radio and heater, we're happy.

The only drawback to keeping our pickups for so long is that we use up most of the remaining trade-in value. My husband is capable of doing the majority of repair work which doesn't cost us a dime, but not everyone shares the same appreciation for custom repairs and parts the way we do. Our pickups might have a unique dashboard knob (i.e.: crimped on brass bullet casing), a little baling wire holding something together, or a heavy duty bolt welded for an inside door handle, but driving something that stands out and puzzles people has never bothered us.

When we're ready to upgrade though, we prefer working with dealerships so we can take advantage of pawning off our old stuff. Trade-ins lessen the out-of-pocket expense to upgrade and our junk yard doesn't fill up with old vehicles this way. When my husband finds a dealership that meets our newer pickup criteria, he'll deal over the phone instead of going there so we can work our trade-in pickup into the purchase before they see it.

He gives the standard make, model, year, and basic under-the-hood information on our potential trade-in and then asks what they'd give us for it. If they want to know what kind of condition the pickup is in, Art applies one of his key trade-in secrets. He chooses wisely his adjectives to describe the trade-in. Our trade-ins always run; they just might not be able to run as fast, as far, or as smoothly, and usually aren't as nice-looking as other trade-ins, so he'll describe the vehicle as "ranchy," but he doesn't bother to clarify what his definition is.

One of his many talents is that when he wants to be persuasive, he picks words that can be interpreted differently by different people. For instance, some dealers think of "ranchy" as a ranch pickup that has more gravel miles than highway miles, has stayed on a ranch during its tenure, is considered more of a work pickup with shoddy-looking seats, or has never been cleaned out or polished with Armor-All car cleaner. Other dealers might envision a very dusty cab and a pickup floor covered with hay, grain, gravel, and dirt amidst ranch-related items. Still others might take "ranchy" to mean that the pickup takes on a manure scent when the floorboards get wet. In our case, "ranchy" means all the above plus rough-looking and ranch-customized. Whatever a dealer envisions, the trade-in value usually changes once it's brought into the dealership.

When it's time to make the sale, the out-of-pocket cost generally ends up being a tad more and our trade-in value a tad less. We usually drive away as satisfied customers anyway. Watching the dealer and shop mechanics' reactions when they see all the custom work on our "ranchy" pickup is always priced right.

My Rancher's First Love

The important events that my rancher-husband remembers with great sentiment can probably be counted on one hand. One of them pertains to his first love.

There are a few moments in our married life that I can't believe my husband doesn't remember with the same importance that I do. He has his own special moments that he remembers such as the day he brought his first girl home. Her name was Samantha.

He was thirteen, and she was from Newell, South Dakota. She was fairly young also but acted mature. Samantha was born and raised a Jersey girl with brown eyes, a tawny gold complexion, and was lactating at the time—she also had some Gurnsey in her.

> **"Your favorite thing: cattle."**
>
> *~Reneé age 6*

Getting Samantha was a time he will always remember because she was the first cow that got him into the cattle business. As a young teenage boy growing up helping his dad with their family's herd, he wanted to start his own cow herd. He saved all of his wages, and he and his dad drove up to Newell in a pickup with a stock rack (remember back when those were still used?) so my husband could buy his first cow. The Jersey-Guernsey cross milk cow cost him about $700 and he named her Samantha.

He took a lot of ribbing about her breed, especially from an elder neighbor down the road, but his pride never wavered. Buying his first cow to establish his own cow herd remains an important milestone in his life.

In all of the 19 years of knowing my rancher-husband, the only times

I've ever seen him get misty-eyed was when his hay fever got to him. There are few things that cause my husband to get emotional—unless of course we're talking about money, ranch work, or maybe even hand signals, but that's an emotion of a different kind for many future columns. Tearing up or showing his emotions is just not something my rancher's walnut-tough exterior will allow him to do. Only females like Samantha have the power to stir up his emotions. I witnessed once just how much buying his first cow meant to him.

It was during a time when he had to endure a court ordeal that pertained to defending the morals of his cowboy way regarding our land and cattle owner rights. When a lawyer asked my husband how long he'd been a rancher, a hairline crack in his stoic facial expression revealed how he truly felt about his cows. He began his response with a long pause at the recollection of Samantha before he said as simply and as quickly as possible with a hint of emotion in his voice; "I bought my first cow when I was thirteen."

Ranchers don't wear their emotions on their sleeves or anywhere else that I'm aware of, but when it comes to livestock, a rancher is protective of the strong ties he has to them. The memories that are created from putting his whole heart and life into livestock everyday are not easily forgotten.

Rare circumstances can cause the most calloused, persevering, hardship-hardened men to reveal a poignant, albeit brief moment of emotion regarding what his cows mean to him. It's something you're not likely to ever see expressed on the faces people advocating humane treatment of animals.

Part II: Kids

Raising Ranch Kids

"We don't have slackers on our ranch." ~Myles age 6

Myles (eating his sandwich from the saddle) and Reneé on Paquito.
(*Photo by Amy Kirk*)

For ranching parents, every day is "Bring Your Child to Work Day." From the time our kids were babies, we've taken them along to our work. They'd get excited about going along if they thought there was a store stop for "coffee" (aka pop and a candy bar) and sometimes there was a lot of bawling and whining going on. On those days they'd get drug along anyway. Some days they didn't have a choice; we had to bring them with us.

I learned how to get creative in keeping our ranch kids occupied in order for my husband and me to feed, check livestock water in the summer, prepare a big meal for our branding crew, move cows horseback, or with me in the feed pickup lead the herd down the back road. Like a normal mother, I got impatient and I did whatever it took to get the job done with cranky kids in tow. As a result, our kids became resilient little buggers who figured out how to entertain themselves.

Whenever they complained about why they had to go do chores and not get to play first, they heard us lecture repeatedly, "We take care of our livestock first before we can do what we want." They also grew up learning, sometimes the hard way, about the golden rules on our ranch: shut the gate, take your muddy boots off at the door, then as teenagers they got, "Don't drive on the grass; that's feed for our cows."

I'm grateful the majority of our kids' child development has taken place outdoors; either by their choice or by ours when ranch chores had to get done—or they were driving me nuts. There's no doubt that our kids know what we do when we go to work because they've got their own responsibilities helping us take care of our livestock.

Family Days

With the exception of a couple years, we've always made the sale day of our calves a family day.

Some years it took every trick in my diaper bag to keep one or both of our kids occupied until our calves sold. The action and noise in the sale ring only entertained them for a little while. The tricks I used to keep them from wanting to running off included nursing or feeding them and a nap, toy cows and pickups, pen and paper or my calculator's buttons. Once we'd sold and got ready to leave, I had to round up all our coats, hats, mittens and baby paraphernalia.

> *"It's like when you collect the eggs but the chickens do all the work."*
>
> *~Myles age 9*

For me, some of the sale days I remember most weren't over how our calves looked or sold, but how disastrous it was with a baby and a preschooler. One memorable sale day, we had to listen to a very unhappy baby in a car seat with a dirty diaper the last couple of miles to the sale barn.

You'd think my husband and I would've learned after one kid disappeared on sale day, to pay closer attention the next time, but both of our kids have gone exploring around the sale barn before. The first time, Art and I got so engrossed watching the calves sell ahead of ours, that we didn't even notice when our 5 year old son wandered off. It turned out our pint-sized cowboy didn't go far. He was in the next room content to talk with other cowboys working in the sale barn about cows while having pie with them for Customer Appreciation Day. Once my panic dissolved, I asked Myles what he was doing and he informed me, "Oh, me an' the guys are just havin' some pie," (even though he didn't know any of their names).

A few years later, it was our daughter's turn. Once again my spouse and I got hypnotized by the auctioneer's voice and fixated on watching other calves sell until ours went through the sale ring. My husband broke out of the stupor first and asked me, "Where's Reneé?" I couldn't believe we'd let it happen again. For a second time, we split up and searched the building. She'd gone to the sale barn café to see if the cashier would give her a candy bar since I told her no earlier.

Sale day has gotten a lot different now that our kids are teenagers. It probably has something to do with the fact that now our kids have their own calf crop to sell. They both wait patiently and sit perfectly still; so much that our son started to doze off one time. It was an odd feeling the first time I got to go to the sale barn without having someone to entertain or go find. While watching calves run through the ring, I've realized I didn't miss much in years past like I thought.

Our kids stay put and gather up all their stuff by themselves now but I've over-trained myself. Even though I don't have to pack a diaper bag around anymore, I haven't gotten over my obsession to constantly be looking for my family members. Nowadays I have to try and figure out where my husband went and who he got sidetracked talking to.

Name That Baby!

When my due date got closer with my first pregnancy, if people asked us whether we wanted a boy or girl, I gave them the standard answer: I just wanted a baby with a name my husband and I agreed on. By the size of me, there was no question the baby would be healthy...and big.

I was disappointed to discover that my husband already had an opinion about our child's name. Picking names wasn't like planning our wedding a few years before, where he let me make all the decisions. I wrongly assumed that his interest in our baby's name would be similar to his interest in deciding on our wedding colors, flowers, the wedding cake, decorations, registering for gifts, and choosing dinnerware. I thought that I'd get to make the baby-naming decision by myself. Instead, when I shared the boys' and girls' names I liked, my husband hastily vetoed them and suggested names he liked, which I vetoed even quicker.

He was also very opinionated about names that sounded like a last name or that he felt belonged to the opposite sex. If it was a boy, he wanted a masculine-sounding, old-fashioned, cowboy name that was easy to spell and pronounce, and wasn't weird or unheard of. He preferred something legendary, like Augustus, our cowboy hero from the western classic, *Lonesome Dove*. "Then we can call 'im (our baby) Gus for short!" I responded much the same way I'm guessing my mother did when my dad wanted to name me "Buck" if I had been a boy.

One holiday, my sister-in-law read names out of the phone book. That's when my husband shared another one of his baby-naming opinions. "It needs to be a one-syllable name that I can yell." My reply was, "We're not naming a dog or a horse, honey!"

As my sister-in-law read off names that fit my husband's criteria, he would practice hollering them out loud to determine their effectiveness when spoken at a holler. He also rhymed names with all the words that he could think of because his own name, Art, became part of a rhyming joke he disliked as a kid.

Furthermore, if it was a boy, my husband said we had to carry on the family naming tradition: making the child's life miserable with his first and middle name. We didn't consider naming a boy "Sue" to make him tough as the Johnny

Cash song "A Boy Named Sue" implied, but rather he would go by his middle name and his first name would be the same as my husband's middle name, Arthur (Art for short which is the name my husband goes by). This was all meant to confuse people—which I'm assuming I've successfully achieved here—over whether the person in question is the dad or the son, and to give the child a lifetime of headaches when filling out paperwork from always having to clarify his given name and the name that he goes by. All of my husband's stipulations made it especially difficult to find a boy's name that we both liked, and not surprisingly, our firstborn was indeed a boy. We did manage to agree on a boy's name my husband could holler in one syllable.

You can imagine how happy I was when our baby arrived and I got what I wanted: a healthy (eight pound, eleven ounce) baby. We call him Myles, but sometimes we holler, "MYLES!"

Ranching Career Trainees

Our kids' instincts to ranch were evident at an early age. They recognized a good incentive package for helping with outside chores over inside ones.

Each milestone they met meant they were on their way to a ranching career. At one and two, our little rancher trainees wanted to go with dad and be just like him. They had toddler-sized work clothes similar to dad's, which further created a yearning to be his apprentice. Our cowkids wore cowboy boots, Carhartt coats, coveralls, silk neckerchiefs, scotch caps or cowboy hats, and Wrangler bungee pants (elastic waist band pants that fit over diapers). Once there was nothing to come between our kids and their Dad, specifically dirty diapers, they easily ditched Mom for a morning with Dad. To our ranchers in training, it meant not only getting to go with dad but, more importantly, stopping for coffee. After riding along checking cows for a little bit, he'd take them to the store to catch up on the local news over an entire can of pop and a candy bar the size of a newborn infant—something that was part of Dad's rancher trainee incentive package that Mom never offered.

Art to Reneé: "To me, if you have one Groovy Girl (doll) that would be enough." Myles: "But you can never have too many cows."

~Myles age 10

From the ages of three to five, they furthered their ranch training by "helping" with chores, checking cows more, and having question-and-answer sessions with Dad on how tractors, windrowers, and balers worked. Sessions lasted until the trainee got bored or fell asleep, usually on the tractor or windrower cab floor.

Art and his clone headed out for some "ranch career training" feeding cows.
(*Photo by Amy Kirk*)

The floor space of our tractors and windrowers have traditionally only had enough room to store an oversized lunch pail but our mini ranchers found enough space to consider the cab floor a cozy fun place to hang out with Dad. When they'd get sleepy they'd just stuff Dad's jacket behind their little heads and amazingly, sleep like that on the rubber-matted floor with their knees scrunched up to the oversized cab window. Many-a-time I pulled up to gather a kid and could only see knobby white kneecaps sticking out of worn out Wranglers or the smooth soles of kid cowboy boots while Dad's buddy slept in the cab.

The end of the nap-taking era was a milestone that meant more independence and less supervision. Our kids didn't have to ride with mom and take a nap in the pickup anymore while moving cows. On branding days, our trainees rode along horseback to help gather and bring in cows instead of watching from the corral fence with mom. They were able to climb saddles by themselves, control their horses, and didn't cry if the horses started to trot off. They could withstand day-long horseback rides pushing cows and didn't have to have their horses tethered to Mom or Dad's saddle horn. They fed bottles to calves, got gates, fetched tools, and "worked" with Dad in the shop. This also signaled the age at which they could drive a pickup in granny low while the flatbed trailer got loaded with square bales for the bulls and horses.

Once our kids reached double digits (between ten and twelve) they were able to see over the steering wheel and their feet could reach the pedals. They could wrestle the smallest baby calves at branding, lift big forkfuls of hay, and operate equipment in the hay field instead of riding along.

Becoming a tween was a milestone for our son that meant he could finally lift, pack, and toss hay bales onto the flatbed trailer and drive a pickup without having to raise his chin in order to see over the dash. He picked out bigger calves to wrestle on branding day and branded his own calves.

Each of these milestones has emphasized the ins and outs of a competitive ranching career. Dad was in because he'd stop for coffee and buy pop and candy bars. Mom was out because she hadn't come up with an incentive package nearly as attractive.

Dress Her Drawers

If you check a cowboy's drawers, you're likely to find a pile of silk scarves and bandanas in at least one of them. Cowboys keep their necks warm with silk scarves and use bandanas as hankies or rags.

My cowboy gets both types of these simple fabric squares as gifts a lot because they are a popular and a safe bet to give cowboys for any gift-giving occasion. Unlike some dads who cringe over getting another tie, cowboy dads use this type of neckwear (also called wild rags, silk rags, or neckerchiefs) regularly as well as hankies and bandanas. My husband keeps his in the top drawer of his dresser but occasionally they get raided.

When our son was little he used his dad's red silk scarves as superhero capes but now he wears them around his neck and packs a hankie in his pocket like his dad. When our daughter discovered them as a toddler, she chose to use them in more creative ways. She favored Dad's silk scarves because of the smooth feel of the material and their 30 inch square size. They're more versatile for playing with compared to bandanas which are only 18 inches square, but she found just as many uses for them also.

"But can I bring some girlie stuff?"(moving cows)
~Reneé age 4

Hankies and silk rags also come in colorful varieties and pretty patterns that attracted her attention. Back when she took naps, her favorite was a bright blue silk rag she used as a blanket. Many a silk rag of her dad's became part of her wardrobe. She'd spend hours playing dress-up using his silk rags and bandanas. I was her tailor for her different custom-requested outfits, tying and pinning them around her body in different ways. My personal favorite is what she used to call a "draggin' dress" in which I tucked a scarf into her underwear around her waist for a skirt that "dragged" behind her. Combining cotton and silk material with mixed colors and different patterns together wasn't as important as being styled the way she envisioned (and she was always an unsatisfied customer if it wasn't).

Dad's old bandanas made useful blankets for her stuffed animals and for swaddling her dolls and babies with or to make a pretend bandage or cast. Bandanas and scarves could be conveniently made into a purse, hobo bag or snack sack with a big holding capacity. She would take them filled with things for entertainment on car rides, to church, or to sporting events. They also hung easily on handlebars when bike riding and packing her supplies needed for a hike or a trip to the tree fort.

The square size made them easy to fold and pack around, but best of all, Dad always had lots of them. If one turned up lost or more were needed to play with, she just went and got another one out of his drawer. He was a good sport about taking all the new, stiff bandanas to break in until they become soft and worn enough for a girl's liking, and he didn't mind using the silk rags with the rips or holes in them.

Even though she'd sometimes empty my husband's hankie and wild rag supply, I'd remind him that eventually she'll outgrow them and when she does he'll miss the days she used to dress her drawers with them.

The Dirt Kicker

Dirt and boys—they just go together. When our son was a toddler, his idea of hitting pay dirt was getting to play with it.

His fascination for fine dry soil started a dirt-kicking phase. It all began when he followed me under the slat-covered porch one day to clean out all the debris that had gathered there. The soft dirt caught his attention as the setting sun highlighted the dust that our feet stirred up. He was as mesmerized as a moth drawn to a lantern. The look on his face of intense interest with the drifting clouds of dust was cute at first, but then his fascination got annoying.

After figuring out that kicking dirt made dust clouds, he became obsessed. The four foot high space underneath the porch was easy for him to run up and down the sloped ground to create a dust storm that eventually ran me out of there. All summer long he kicked dirt under the porch, and it was like having Pigpen of the Peanuts Gang living with us.

Kicking dirt consumed our boy as if it were his job. Everyday for hours at a time he HAD to go under the porch from the moment he woke up and got his ball cap and bib overalls on so he could roust dirt.

He'd run up the slope, stop to watch the dust float away then run back and watch it again. The more time he spent under the porch, the more he perfected his technique to produce bigger dirt clouds around his feet before it drifted away. He discovered wearing his grey, fake alligator skin cowboy boots accomplished this quite well. They became his dirt kicking boots. Nothing stirred up dust like those grey hand-me-downs. He'd drag his foot inward like he was pigeon toed as he ran, for maximum dirt fluffing, and he wore them everywhere in case he found dirt to kick around at other places.

I had to bathe him daily after he did his dirt work. Fine grit would cling to his sweaty little body and he always felt sticky when he came in. His forehead would have a black horizontal line where he wore his cap from dirt mixing with his sweaty wet hair and he had black rings around his lips and nose, and grime in his ears.

Besides kicking it, he liked to have an audience watch him work the dirt. He'd pester whoever was around to come and watch him. He was a loyal dirt kicker who loved his job and didn't need much supervising when no one was around to spectate. I would just occasionally peek over the porch to see if dirt was still coming out from under it while cooking dinner or working in the house.

Once he discovered this fine dust, he was constantly checking out dirt in other places like the barn, wallows that cows frequented, soft spots in driveways and other people's dirty shop floors. One time he stirred up the dust in an elder rancher's shop so bad that the he finally shouted, "STOP KICKIN' THAT DIRT!"

It wasn't long after that he grew out of his grey cowboy boots and his dirt kicking phase. I didn't miss the hassle his phase caused as I tried to keep him and his clothes clean before having to go somewhere. I just missed the dirt cheap entertainment that it provided.

Reneé getting some kid therapy on the tire swing. (*Photo by Amy Kirk*)

Kid Therapy

I've been sending my kids to therapy regularly for a long time now. I've insisted on it since they were babies.

After spending too many consecutive days indoors, my kids will relapse into zoo-like behavior, a sign that they need some therapy. Like a woman waiting too long before re-dying her hair, their behavior becomes very unattractive and hard to ignore. They get hyperactive and run around the house or want to play outside games inside, and the frequency of their bickering escalates. They whine or complain about doing chores, get impatient, and have fits when something they're trying to fix or make doesn't work. They'll also frequently display short-temperedness.

> *"Now I'm gonna power up that swing!"*
>
> ~*Myles age 7*

They like what their therapist does to help them handle daily stress and benefit from her services every time they visit. She has a way of making therapy enjoyable and my kids anticipate future visits. You may have heard of their therapist because she's known worldwide. She goes by the name of Mother Nature and was my therapist as a kid also. She's kind of old-school in her treatment strategies, but that is also the reason why I like her.

The type of therapy my kids receive often encourages using their five senses. Okay, maybe not tasting so much anymore, but that was an important sense to them their first year when they wanted to know what sand, grass, bugs, rocks, and dirt tasted like. Many of their sessions also involve interaction with animals which might include running around with the family dog, Pepper, finding, catching, and petting the barn kittens, or riding horses.

Mother Nature encourages them to use their imagination, be themselves (or somebody else if they choose), explore new ideas, exercise their bodies—often in the form of serious energy burning—and their minds. I like it that her office is not conducive to overstimulation. They get just enough stimulation to occupy their curious minds for long periods of time. It's a particularly productive session if they go to therapy clean and come home dirty—often a big part of their visits. Whenever a lot of progress is made, they're usually too tired to fight or complain about anything at the end of the day, which helps them sleep at night, too.

My kids have never had a bad therapy session, unless not being able to go counts. They're always eager to share with me the exciting things they discovered, learned, or did, and come back refreshed and happy.

I also like that my kids' therapist listens and allows them to discover and figure things out for themselves using their original thoughts. She doesn't find it necessary to take over but lets them carry out their own ideas. Her office is a safe place to be creative, learn, wonder, challenge, question, find out, experiment, and explore. As a busy parent, I find a perk to Mother Nature's services to be her availability. Her door's open 24/7 and she takes walk-ins.

What I love most about Mother Nature is her expertise in dealing with the boredom syndrome, which is quite common among children. Take it from me, if you have kids with boredom syndrome, call on Mother Nature. She'll see them right away and has an uncanny way of treating the problem in a day.

"Miracle wire" saved on a gate leftover from feeding square bales to our horses.
(*Photo by Amy Kirk*)

Miracle Wire

For a while, our son was convinced his dad made miracles happen. As a two-year old, he believed baling wire produced miracles because his dad used it a lot and called it "miracle wire."

The nickname stuck with our son because he witnessed baling wire saving the day many times when my husband made a lot of farm and ranch toys work again that wouldn't hold up to rough play. Dad's miracle wire replaced broken toy trailer hitches and attached accessories to the tricycle, hot wheels, and little bike. It also added a cowboy ambiance to the tree fort. My husband bent and manipulated a piece of baling wire into whatever was necessary to meet a kid's desire and could get our boy back to playing in no time.

Our pint-sized cowboy learned early on that baling wire is an important staple on our ranch. He spent a lot of time going with his dad and saw how miracle wire could be used in place of any tool, if the right equipment wasn't brought along. When he didn't think broken fence wires or gates could be repaired, my husband eased his mind and demonstrated how baling wire miraculously repairs a fence. Dad showed him how to splice broken wire, anchor it to wooden posts, replace fencing staples and clips, or loop it to make a new gate latch if an old one gave out. Our son was along a lot of the time when a fence was spotted that needed fixing and he watched or "helped out." Our future rancher also learned that miracle wire could be a temporary fix to buy some time, or a permanent one, since baling wire can hold up so dang long.

As an inquisitive toddler, our son asked a lot of questions and always wanted to help or talk about whatever his dad was working on. I wasn't surprised when he tried to help fix a windmill at a livestock tank. My husband and father-in-law needed to get it working again, and junior and I went along.

I stayed at the pickup with our son, while the guys tried to figure out how to get the windmill running again and listened to them vent their frustrations at each other over the problem. To avoid making the situation worse, I kept our little man occupied with the junk banked up in the corners of the pickup box until his dad and grandpa were able to come up with a solution. The ruckus between the guys over the situation escalated, and I was hoping that our son was too busy with his findings to notice. He kept showing me little rocks and pop tabs he'd found, and stuffed them into his bib overall pockets; *then* he spotted a wad of baling wire.

He pulled it out of the debris, held it up in the air, and spoke a quote of inspiration for the day: "DAD! I got some miracle wire for ya!"

Fixes and Kisses

When our kids were small, they knew better than to come to me with their broken toys or equipment. The best I could do was give kids a sympathetic hug or a kiss, but neither were successful at repairing their toys.

My approach didn't "fix it," or do much to make the kids feel better, but my husband delighted in reversing their frustration over their broken toys. He'd tell them all the time, "Dad can fix anything," and he proved that there was nothing he couldn't fix, by welding on their run-over bike frames or broken swings, and using duct tape or baling wire whenever possible to fasten toy parts back together. Our kids never walked away with their repair items disappointed. My husband always got great satisfaction out of seeing big smiles on their faces when he'd hand them something he repaired, because he hated to see them sad over broken toys or equipment; he is a habitual fixer on this place. He would go to great lengths to see the kids' (or mine) looks of amazement at his work. I marveled at the sight of him at the kitchen table one time sewing up a ripped stuffed animal for our daughter.

One day she came home from kindergarten very distraught. She'd told her friends at school, "My dad can fix anything!" and no matter how much she tried to convince them she was telling the truth, they didn't believe her. When she relayed the scene to us at the supper table, my husband reassured her that he did, in fact, know how to fix anything by recounting a list of things he'd already fixed for her. He stated that she's just lucky because "Those other girls have never had me fix their stuff and don't know what I can do."

As if he held some sort of doctorate in toy-repairing, he said, "Some dads' solution is to just go buy another one, especially if they don't have the knowledge, education, and training to fix stuff like I do," which produced a giggle and a smile. As she regained confidence in his abilities, he added, "Town dads probably don't know how to fix things the way I can because they've never seen what baling wire, electrical tape, duct tape, gorilla glue, or a welder can do."

Making repairs on a ranch is a year-round job that requires imaginative thinking in problem solving since conventional solutions never seem readily available, and don't always hold up as well or as long, but more importantly because we're better at improvising than spending money. Our outfit readily keeps my husband's "fixit" skills fine-tuned. By the looks of some of the repair jobs he's done for our kids, I'd say he's overqualified. Our kids' ranch-style fixit jobs may not always look pretty when they get their stuff back but they'll definitely be fixed.

I always felt helpless as a mother when my kids would bring me their broken things and I didn't know how to repair them. I've always been thankful and relieved whenever my husband fixed anything kid-related. If my standard hug-and-a-kiss fix-it solution wouldn't do the job, I would turn to my husband to restore their childhood happiness. Whenever I don't know how to fix something that their dad can AND make our kids happy again, I give him a big thank you hug and a kiss.

The Golden Rule

As parents, my husband and I do our best to teach our kids about the dangers and consequences of drugs, alcohol, and not shutting gates.

We persistently preach the golden rule at our house: SHUT THE GATE. Unfortunately, our kids usually don't comprehend the full import of our words until they experience for themselves the consequences of leaving a gate open. There's no better way to grasp this concept than when they have a friend or two over who leave a gate open and they get reprimanded for their friends' mistakes. Such instances result in our kids learning that breaking our golden rule has the severest consequence of any careless act.

Our golden rule takes priority over all others because carelessness with gates affects not only the culprit but all the innocent livestock that get out and all the family members (if help is needed) who have to drop what they are doing in order to help gather the wayward animals, which can sometimes be a challenge. Open gates can be an invitation to a livestock disaster. The repercussions have the potential to be fatal to livestock depending on what feed the cows or horses got into and gorged themselves on and how long they've been eating it.

We put a lot of effort into instilling good work ethics, good character-building qualities and good morals in our kids, essentially so my husband and I don't have to do additional work, specifically, work that could've been avoided. As land, livestock, and gate owners, we deal with other people's negligence going through our gates enough as it is, so we try to eliminate such carelessness with our kids.

Where a kid comes from and what level of common sense he or she has can be determined by the way that kid handles a gate he or she encounters. Hardcore country kids are easy to identify because they subconsciously shut gates behind them. This is likely because they've experienced post-traumatic open-gate stress disorder at their own place. My husband and I are adamant that shutting gates becomes a well established habit in our kids so we can be confident that they will close gates behind them when they visit other people's yards, farms, and especially ranches. It's our goal to raise exemplary citizens who have common sense enough to close any gates they open, wherever they go.

We expect them to be positive influences on their peers and set good examples of gate-closing for their friends who may visit us. We also encourage our kids to openly share horror stories of what has happened when gates were found left open at our place so that the traumatic tales they tell of their parents' fury will stick with friends who may encounter a gate some day—especially if the gates happen to be ours.

The outcome of non-country kids' gate mistakes end up being an experience of a lifetime I doubt our son and daughter will ever forget. Numerous times our kids have had to deal with the consequences of their friends' negligence when our family has had to gather animals that got out as a result of one of their friends leaving a gate open. We've had to round up horses that got through an open man-gate and were grazing in our uncut alfalfa field and another time cows were found helping themselves to the round bales in the hay yard after they discovered that the gate was left wide open. A wild cow that we had in a corral and was scheduled for processing, escaped through a gate left open and was difficult to get back in. The biggest lesson our kids have learned from gates being left open is: CHOOSE FRIENDS WISELY.

Checking water tanks is a daily chore during the summer months. Myles and Reneé are often a part of range checking if not in charge of it at times.
(Photo by Amy Kirk)

Ranch Kid Boot Camp

The way our kids are raised isn't much different than military boot camp: lots of hollering, hustling, and having to take orders.

The first skill our kids acquired after learning to walk, was knowing how to hustle. It didn't take them long to figure out that being fast and efficient was the ideal way to do their work and ours, if they didn't want to be hollered at. They instinctively do everything swiftly now because doing so is highly praised.

The reason why we call our children "dependents" is simple: we depend on them to do the tasks that we put them in charge of despite assigning them jobs beyond their age level or lifting capabilities. After our kids joined our family "unit," they had to start taking orders. We told them to. They now know that we expect a lot from them: to be all they can be plus everything we can be and more. As a result, they are becoming well-trained country

> *"I'm in charge of everything that goes wrong."*
> *~Myles age 15*

kids.

Experiencing failure is expected whether at military boot camp or ranch boot camp, and when our kids make mistakes they learn something from each mistake: they're going to get chewed out. Over the years they've come to expect a certain degree of yelling, and they know how to take it. Verbal barrages callous them for the real world and some bosses. Our ranch style parenting has trained our kids to get used to working in intense circumstances, being critiqued on how to do a job right, getting yelled at when they mess up, but always getting a second chance to do it right—all worthy experiences for coping in stressful situations.

Their assigned ranch work has prepared them to expect the worst and consider it the norm. This is so they aren't disappointed when their high expectations such as getting the same treatment as other kids, aren't met. Our kids not only rely on each other when one of them is under parental attack but have experienced the value of team work because they aren't going to get out of helping the rest of the family unit.

They've also come to assume the unexpected and be prepared for it. They know cows, weather, equipment, their parents' moods, or changes in their plans all contribute to reinforcing their learning opportunities.

It didn't take our kids more than ten years to figure out that life is better when they think ahead and take the initiative to do what needs done and to always "look busy." It equals less yelling. This coincides with being expected to think quickly on their feet, which benefits their life-skills to survive on their own because quick-thinking gets praised.

In the barracks on the Kirk ranch there isn't much sleeping in, but during the summertime, after a full day of putting up hay for instance, they don't have problems sleeping once they're allowed to, and they eat good because they're kept busy all day. Our young troopers also know how to adapt to diverse environments. They're accustomed to sleeping on hard ground and consider it an enjoyable activity to partake in our front yard every summer.

When they graduate from high school, we know they'll do just fine being able to handle the real world. If they decide to join the military, their ranch-raised background will come in handy—they'll just be grandfathered in.

Fair Enough

Participating in our county fair is fun unless you're a 4-Her. I turn into the Wicked Witch of the Fair when it gets down to the wire with my kids and their 4-H projects.

The weeks prior to Achievement Days, I have to look at or walk around posters and displays propped up against unused spaces during their varied stages of completion. It doesn't help my mood that our fair is during the Sturgis Motorcycle Rally (where Harley Davidson motorcycle enthusiasts from all over the nation meet for a weeklong partyfest) and the most commonly used route to get to our fairgrounds winds through Custer State Park. The drive over starts out enjoyable, but getting to the fair on time quickly turns stressful. Driving with motorcycles swarming on all sides of my vehicle like mosquitoes sours a good mood fast. The motorcycle noise sounds like some annoying kid holding down the six lowest organ keys on the biggest cathedral organ outside my window the whole 35 minute drive.

Early in the 4-H year, I start out excited and have good intentions of getting our kids to begin their projects, but nobody, including myself, thinks about projects or gets seriously motivated until a month beforehand. By July, persistent nagging to get started, work on, or finish projects echoes throughout the house. Once the effectiveness of regular naggings wears off, other equally effective tactics are used. This includes but is not limited to: guilt-tripping, slave-driving, privilege-revoking, or escalated harping.

Guilt-tripping is when a parent (the mom) puts the 4-Her(s) on a guilt trip for not working on their projects, especially if the kids hold offices in their 4-H club and are expected to set an example for other members. Slave-driving is getting the 4-Hers up early, and the entire day's agenda is project work. Escalated harping is a mild term for yelling and/or arguing over project work or lack thereof. Revoking privileges--like being a kid, going with Dad, or visiting a friend--happens when projects are still not done and 72 hours remain before J-Day (project judging).

I'm ashamed to admit I've resorted to using all of these strategies out of desperation to get my kids to complete their projects. But what kind of "involved" parent would I be if I allowed my kids to show up at the fair with incomplete projects or none at all? It would reflect badly on my involvement if I didn't do my part and crack the whip.

The problem lies in the fact that I persuaded my children to take certain projects I felt were life skills they needed to learn and agreed to help them brainstorm spectacular project ideas, and that's where it remained until fair time. Getting my kids to complete their projects year-round would be the life skill I need to learn about.

I'm confident our fair established Saturday night's event specifically for parents like me to have something to look forward to after kids get their projects to Achievement Days. It's the kind of event that takes away the edginess of fair tensions, offers something to get through the rest of the fair, and is highly anticipated by fair-going adults every year. Once I've gotten my kids and all their projects delivered intact and I've had my fill of contending with distracted vacationers' driving, motorcycle traffic, grandstand seating, and concession stand meals, Saturday night's annual Beers 'N Ears distracts me from the stresses I let override my fair-time fun.

The kids get premiums for their projects and I get steaming sweet corn and a frosty mug of beer. Now that's fair.

Monopolizing the Game

My son loves board games and I'm not talking about the fun, enjoyable ones. I'm talking about the torturous kinds that take so long to end that they require breaking for meals and bedtime. You know, like Monopoly.

Not having satellite, cable, or local television at our house is partially to blame for my son's Monopoly obsession. Monopoly is one of those games that either you love or you hate. There's really no in-between. I don't love it—there's definitely no in-between.

Monopoly is a game for people who possess a unique characteristic known as "patience." I'm partial to games that can be over in less time than it takes to travel to New Jersey from South Dakota. Regardless of how quickly I let my Monopoly money run out, it can still feel like a game of infinity. My son is the only one in our family who truly finds the game enjoyable.

> **"Let's calm ourselves down and play a board game."**
>
> *- Reneé age 9*

Our Monopoly game is usually hard to get to mostly because I see to it that it is out of sight, but sometimes he actually moves stuff around to find it if he really wants to play. I used to secretly invite family down just so he had new people to talk into playing Monopoly besides us. No matter how tough it got to recruit players, his grandmothers were always dependable suckers.

He developed various ways to get hesitant people to play or continue playing, using his Monopoly modifications in addition to the game's fast play rules. His biggest Monopoly playing year was back in 2008. He single-handedly kept my mom in a game after inventing the U.S. Government edition known as the "Bailout" version. It enabled Grandma to keep playing when she ran out of money too soon and ended the game in less than four hours. Government Bailout Monopoly has since become a favorite version among extended family members wanting to experience getting money handouts as consequences to corrupt investing.

Another time when our kids spent a week with their other grandmother, my son was so desperate for his sister and their grandma to play Monopoly with him that he was willing to let sister play Monopoly via Grandma's phone intercom system. She agreed to play from the third floor loft while he and Grandma played out on the deck. This allowed little sister freedom to hang out in the loft and have an excuse to use the intercom while appeasing my son's desire for an all afternoon Monopoly game. Whenever it was sister's turn, Monopoly Dictator would call her on the intercom, roll the dice for her, draw the necessary cards, and advise her on her options. She would then intercom her game-playing decision, permitting him to manage her money for transactions.

In lean times back home, when lenient game rules wouldn't even sway resistant family members to participate, he had to reinvent the game. During the Monopoly Depression era he was so desperate he would be other players and play against himself. For several months that winter I had to walk around a perpetual Monopoly game spread out on his bedroom floor.

Playing Monopoly may not be my preferred way to spend my free time but I'd still rather be talked into playing Monopoly by the standard rules than have to tolerate being exposed to one episode of dim-witted reality TV programming.

One of the Kirk family's cattle brands; now passed on to Myles and Reneé for their cow herd. (*Photo by Amy Kirk*)

My Brand

A brand and a signature are both distinctive forms of identification, but a rancher's pride is seeing his brand on the cows he owns. Some cattlemen like their brands more than their signatures.

> *"I see a brand on that heifered one."*
>
> *-Myles age 7*

Our son is no different than older ranchers with their brands. Myles inherited his grandfather's brand as a nine year old and his fondness for it shows. Over the years, it's been graffitied inside hats and jackets, notebooks and personal items of value. He carved it on trees, barn timbers, wooden corral panels and posts or drew it in the dirt on pickups.

His signature used to get the attention of his grade school teachers when he'd put his name *and* brand on his assignments. Marking items with his brand also came in handy for identifying the owner when I found things I didn't know who they belonged to.

In grade school, Myles was the kind of kid who stood out anyway. I could easily spot him amongst his classmates in Fall and Winter because he was the only one who wore a scotch cap, canvas chore coat, and lace-up overshoes (he liked wearing overshoes for their "ranchier" look instead of snow boots).

Since ranching is not the predominant industry in this area, ranch kids aren't hard to spot. People would notice and comment on our eleven-year old whenever he wore his silverbelly cowboy hat in public. He has always been proud to wear it, for by doing so, he makes a statement that he comes from a ranch.

Our country boy mastered hand-eye coordination skills as a kid by calf-roping or card-shuffling, and he liked strategizing how to beat his dad at gin, cribbage, blackjack, or chess. Myles has always preferred outside activities and used to read the *Farmer's Almanac* regularly to learn about weather patterns and forecasts.

"Doing homework is kind of like riding a bronc. You gotta stay on top."

~Myles age 12

This brand of kid seldom gets bored because my husband and I quickly recruit his help on our work if being a kid gets boring. Since he grew up spending a lot of time helping his dad in the shop repairing equipment and welding on ranch projects, he can identify and use most of the shop's tools and equipment and knows how to rely on baling wire to fix stuff.

He knows his parents expect nothing less than being responsible and showing respect and helpfulness toward others. I have always looked forward to picking him up from a friend's or attending parent-teacher conferences so I can get the dirt on what he's like away from home, but when other adults compliment his behavior and helpfulness, I smile, thank them, and say to myself, "That's my brand."

Take Your Pick

Every farm and ranch kid has had to pick his or her fair share of rocks. Rocks in hay fields are God's way of building character in kids.

Each rock that gets picked out of a hay field is one less spewing tirade over broken section teeth that have to be replaced on the windrower before cutting hay can be resumed. Once a hay field has been cut, baled, and bales cleared off, rocks are easier to spot. Rock pickers may believe they've picked a field clean of every stone but hay fields are never rock-free. The U. S. national debt will be eliminated long before the rocks on our hay ground are gone because every summer a new crop of rocks shows up enabling generations of young, energetic kids to experience picking rocks out of a field.

Not all kids get paid to pick rock, but my husband and I are willing to use money as an incentive for our kids, so it's a win-win. If they aren't interested in picking rock to earn money, then they can pick rock anyway and we'll keep the money.

After haying the field by our house one summer day, our daughter was interested in earning money picking rock. The job paid ten dollars a pickup load and she wanted to do all the work herself. She envisioned earning a quick $100 if she got ten loads in one day. The Augustus McCrae in me wanted to say, "Yer in over your head, Pete," because it's always been my experience that quick money-making schemes usually pay better in hard-learned lessons than in fast cash, but who was I to squash her dreams? There were plenty of rocks that needed picking.

By early afternoon and two and a half pickup loads of rock later, sister strolled up to the house disgruntled and discouraged by the lack of speed with which she was able to get a pickup load. The only hayed field that was ready to harvest rock from wasn't the bumper crop she imagined and each load took longer than she expected.

I wanted to help her reach her goal, but being a sympathetic takeover mom has never been one of my strong points. Plus, I knew it wouldn't be as gratifying to her if I helped. I prefer taking over when it's something I'm interested in. Instead I gave her some helpful pointers and a five gallon bucket to speed up the rock-gathering process. By the end of the day she hadn't met her goal, but the rock hunting experience provided her with some good lessons:

1. Get started early. The hay field isn't shaded.
2. Do as much as possible the first day. Ambition dwindles drastically by the second day.
3. It's the only such job a kid is completely in charge of doing.
4. Such work manifests ingenuity in figuring out a more efficient system for getting the job done.
5. It looks like an easy job until you want to make some quick cash doing it.
6. Picking up rocks is a humbling job, but it's also motivational. I have a feeling she'll be a lot more persistent in getting a college degree.

A Ranch Kid's Rite of Passage

Calf wrestling has been a rite of passage for my son. His journey toward the goal of becoming a "top hand" calf wrestler began in my lap.

It was at the feisty age of three that he caught the calf wrestling fever associated with late spring. He wanted to be just like his dad: do men's work, be tough, and drink beer. I'm kidding of course. We wouldn't allow him to do men's work until he was of age—around eight. Pop held priority over beer for him at that age, but his determination to wrestle calves was more persistent, especially when told he wasn't big enough to do it by himself yet.

His early calf wrestling lessons began while I struggled to keep him occupied and tried to distract him from getting in harm's way. I would explain and point out what the guys were doing when they wrestled a calf but had to constantly remind him that he could get hurt because calves can kick hard and run over wrestlers. Upon hearing all of this he decided he wanted to get his own bruises, thus receiving his entitlement to the ranch sport's badge of honor.

Having to watch the action from my lap and the safety of my arms didn't cut it for him. My word of caution only made him more eager to experience branding's contact sport for himself. Occasionally my husband would come get our little man to help hold down a calf. All the while, my husband coached our son on technique and gave numerous tips, pointers, and his high expectations for wrestling calves. He also whispered and pointed out other wrestlers' mistakes as examples of what not to do.

When our boy was six or seven, we'd let him partner up with one of us on the runt calves. My husband would critique his technique and stress the importance of never letting a calf get up until everything's been done first to avoid someone getting hurt or the calf getting away.

Once our youngster got some sand in his back pockets, my husband raised the bar. At twelve years old, our cowboy-in-training was expected to pass up the little calves and go after the big ones. He was repeatedly told that Kirks take on the big calves. Despite being outweighed by some of the calves, wrestling them signified being able to handle his end of a calf. This was the age when our boy realized that calf wrestling was a lot more challenging and entertaining than wrestling his little sister.

When his wrestling abilities and body strength developed, we emphasized the importance of earning the respect of other ranchers and having a reputation for being good help. Under my husband's guidance, our budding calf wrestler quickly learned that the demand for being good help was what builds up a "clientele" with more branding invitations. Since being able to drive, he has broadened his calf wrestling experience and availability, and come late Spring he looks forward to spending weekends making what he calls "the branding circuit."

In what feels like a short time, he's finally gotten big enough to be a calf wrestler who can hold his own but is too big for my lap.

Three-year old Reneé bottle feeding Annabelle; Reneé and Myles' first bucket calf and the heifer calf that started their cow herd. (*Photo by Amy Kirk*)

Raising Country Kids

Kids raised in the country get to work at an early age. Art and I started preparing our kids for the realities of the great outdoors of the rural world when they were small.

A lot of their potty training took place outside. It was necessary since much of our kids' time would be spent going with Mom or Dad to help do chores nowhere near a bathroom. Both of our kids learned to make do wherever nature called them. Convincing our country boy to use the public restrooms when they were available was a little more challenging. In his mind peeing outside was tons quicker in critical moments. We also taught our children to drive at an early age, and not just any vehicles but manual transmission vehicles—the prerequisite to driving ranch equipment so they'd be able to help us out.

We've raised our kids in run-mode because they're expected to know how to move quickly when circumstances make timing vital. Getting a cow in, getting hay put up before it rains, sorting off cows, getting or manning gates, are instances of critical moments when hustling can determine whether a task is a success or failure. Early on, our kids understood what "HUSTLE" and "HURRY UP" means: avoid wasting Dad's time.

Our kids have never said "no" when asked if they'd like to help. They've always been informed what they're going to do. On our ranch everyone is expected to do his or her fair share of men's work regardless of age, gender, current activity, plans, or social status. Sharing the workload is part of being a family on any chain gang.

The number one rule we've branded into our kids' impressionable young heads is to always *shut the gate*. The consequences of leaving a gate open and the risk of livestock getting out is more severe than leaving a house unlocked, giving out their social security number or divulging personal information.

Another one of the rules has to do with our cows' feed supply. Unless it's been recently hayed, our kids have been taught not to drive on hay fields or pastures to avoid killing grass that's intended to feed cows.

Art: (referring to playing with toys as a child.) "Didn't we make you one of those button yo-yos?"
Myles: "Nope. It was all work."

~Myles age 14

My husband has always made sure each of our kids knows how to properly wear a cowboy hat. He considers it a disgrace to the cowboy way when cowboy hats are worn backwards or look appallingly shapeless. He's also instructed them in correctly putting their hats away. Never under any circumstances, should a cowboy hat set on a bed (unless it belongs to a mean bully). A cowboy hat on a bed is bad luck. The day our son learned about this superstition I thought he'd left a gate open somewhere by the reprimanding I overheard him getting about the potential for bad luck.

There's something about ranch work that brings out the loud voice in many frustrated ranchers. Fortunately, our country kids have mastered how to take a scolding like a Marine. When it's time for our kids to leave our ranch boot camp, we're confident they'll leave with good heads on their shoulders. We just hope when they enter the real world, their hats are on straight.

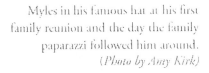

Myles in his famous hat at his first
family reunion and the day the family
paparazzi followed him around.
(Photo by Amy Kirk)

Eluding the Family Reunion Paparazzi

Everybody loves cowboys; especially when they're cute and wearing cowboy boots, black cowboy hats, Wrangler jeans with elastic waistbands, and diapers. The older ladies especially, go crazy for these types.

As a young mother, I witnessed the paparazzi pursuing a cowboy of this nature. My son fell victim to persistent photographers at a very young age when he attended his second family reunion. He became a high profile family reunion attendee at a year and a half old. When he walked by camera-wielding relatives in his black Stetson hat, he quickly established a strong following and was highly pursued the rest of the day. Several extended family members hadn't met our son before, and, apparently, seeing a real cowboy in miniature was a special treat for them.

Being so young and minimally exposed to large crowds, he was completely unprepared for the magnitude of his popularity at the annual gathering. It was the hat. It got him attention he didn't want. The cute little cowboy with chubby cheeks in the black Stetson hat was the talk of the whole reunion.

Eluding people like his Dad and me was a fairly new activity for our son, but during the family reunion he honed the art of escaping when over-stimulation began to take effect and ladies approached him. After meeting numerous strangers who he was told were his relatives, he would try to escape during introductions and had learned how to quicken his pace in his getaways. The whole day his legs hardly stopped moving away from people.

Smiling relatives—mostly women—kept their cameras ready in case they got him to look in their direction. Getting his picture taken quickly annoyed him, and he didn't like ladies he barely knew following him around, asking him questions, or calling his name repeatedly to take his picture wearing his signature cowboy hat. There was no escaping them, cameras or ladies. Women wanted to get a picture with our little cowboy as a memento, but he was not fan club friendly. He had never been exposed to such attention and by late afternoon, showed signs of buckling from the pressure of so many fans.

"GEEZ! Would ya stop with the Myles thing!"

~Myles age 7

The family paparazzi couldn't help themselves. They couldn't get enough of our child's cowboy cuteness, especially when his Dad or grandpa put him on the miniature ponies or the buggy that was brought to the reunion for the kids. All the extra attention has since made him become uncooperative for family-gathering pictures. Many reunion photos show our son fleeing from the group or his Dad holding his crumpled body by his armpits and our son wearing a disgruntled look on his face.

The paparazzi are notorious for getting the better of high profile people and can cause superstars to behave in ways they wouldn't under normal circumstances. Our son was no different. He agreed to a rehabilitative nap in order to restore peace and energy in his life.

At the most recent family reunion, our now teenage son eluded his long-time followers by making arrangements to be somewhere else that day. His loyal fans grilled me on his current status, interests, and whereabouts. One fan brought up the time our boy wore his Stetson hat. When it comes to fame, you can hide from a camera, but you can't escape what's relative.

Part III: Ranch Life

The Lifestyle of the Ranching Family
"I'm just learning as I go." ~Myles Age 4

Myles and Reneé trailing cows out to summer range—a common view on cow-moving day. This picture captures perfectly why it's my favorite day of the ranching calendar year. (*Photo by Amy Kirk*)

Raising a family on a ranch creates a lifestyle all its own. Being distant from grocery and hardware stores, society, and school is expensive, time-consuming, and inconvenient for rural families like ours. Not being able to go to town for every little thing forces us to be more self-sufficient and to rely more on the resources we have around us. Our family is also tougher for having to endure setbacks, hardships, disappointments, and tough challenges we deal with on a regular basis.

"Myles, don't be surprised if I'm mad at you."

~ Reneé age 4

In addition to caring for livestock and managing a herd, we face unexpected ranch-related problems with fences, watering systems, and equipment that have to be addressed immediately. This is why we have our very own junk yard. Many of the things stored at the junk yard are resurrected later to improve upon a current system, solve a problem, or help fulfill a need. Whether it's a better system to make filling feed buckets easier and safer, a wider surface area on the flatbed trailer to haul more round bales, a faster way to haul a calf to the barn with the ATV, or a heavier-duty trailer for hauling water, the first place my husband looks for useable materials is the junk yard.

Compared to conventional families immersed in society and conveniences, we live unconventionally. Our family is used to doing without and being innovative when things like equipment parts, baking ingredients, and socializing are not as easy to obtain as they are for families living in town. We live out one of the Marine Corps' mottos every day: "Improvise, Adapt, Overcome," because we are always having to do one of these if not a combination of them regularly. When I compare how we perceive and apply problem-solving solutions to the way other families would resolve a similar situation, the results can be amusing.

Art: "Where'd you come up with that?"
Reneé: "My witty little brain."

~Reneé age 9

How to Know If Agriculture Has Consumed Your Life

Farmers and ranchers get into their work so much that it can become more than just a job. It can become their whole life. The following list can help you determine if agriculture has taken over your life:

1. Going on a date with your spouse involves "a quick drive" through an implement dealership to look at a tractor or implement.
2. You have 2,536 pairs of gloves scattered in vehicles, tractors, the shop, barn, and house.
3. You own a generator.
4. At least one outbuilding is twice the size of your home.
5. All of your winter coats and caps advertise lick tubs, seed companies, sale barns, implement dealerships, or your preferred source for bulls.
6. A toothpick holder always sets on the kitchen table but you still carry loose toothpicks in your shirt pocket, hat, pickup, and tractor.
7. Your vehicles are licked clean by livestock.
8. Family vacations are centered around county or state fair, farm and ranch shows, stock shows, agricultural conferences or conventions.
9. When your teenage son's buddies show up, you see "an instant work crew"—for free.
10. When the floorboards of your pickup get wet, the cab smells like cake, grain, manure, calves, or hay.
11. You and your spouse were shivareed on your wedding night.

"We went to the bull store." (sale barn)

~Reneé age 4

12. Come November or December you justify buying the equipment you've been mulling over, for tax deduction purposes.
13. FFA and/or 4-H are currently, or were, a part of your life.
14. Your kids' teacher taught you or your spouse in grade school.
15. You've invested more money in equipment than in your house.
16. You plow your own road in the winter.
17. You'll simultaneously drive a tractor or combine while eating lunch or dinner so you don't lose any time even though you eat it all in 1.2 minutes.

18. You're raising your family in the same house you grew up in or that your grandparents lived in when you were a kid.

"I'm a veteran of a lot of wrecks."

~Myles age 12

19. It is of utmost importance that your tractor, combine, or swather/windrower has a working radio.
20. You're a preferred Schwan's customer.
21. You get a discount on auto insurance due to the number of vehicles you own.
22. You consolidate date nights with farm or ranch supply shopping.
23. The reason you get home after 2 a.m. is because you stayed in the field to finish baling, planting, or combining.
24. You check the weather at least twice a day.
25. The number of vehicles, trucks, and trailers you get licensed every year is two pages long.
26. When you go out for supper with your spouse, you have to check a pasture, field, water tank, or gate on the way.
27. Your spouse is from your hometown or a neighboring town.
28. You've had plants sprout on the floorboards of your pickup before.
29. You have a bigger insurance policy on your crops than you do on your home.
30. A long day on the job is when the radio isn't working.
31. Even though you could have an inside job that's less stressful and less laborious, pays better, has better benefits, pays you while on vacation and for holidays that you don't have to work on, you still prefer your job on the farm or ranch.

If you're guilty of any of the aforementioned statements, that's a good sign for agriculture and the economy. It means there will be plenty of opportunities for other people to do all those jobs that farmers and ranchers don't want.

Ranch Hazards

One of the biggest hazards of dealing with livestock everyday is the risk of someone getting his or her clothes damaged.

Ranches are full of clothing hazards. One of these occurs when operating recently greased equipment. Even lightly brushing against grease-exposed parts can achieve this. These menacing stains are especially difficult to remove on my husband's clothes because pre-existing grease stains make it hard to determine old stains from the new ones that could be pre-treated prior to washing—if I were the type to remember to do that.

Another clothing hazard is welding or being exposed to exhaust systems and other mechanical parts that burn and melt things like the synthetic outerwear material of my husband's pricey Carhartt Extreme Arctic coat and coveralls. The most common ranch hazard to clothing, though, is the type of enclosing structure used to contain livestock, called barbwire fencing. Barbwire is more commonly known for its ability to initiate perfectly good, intact clothing into ranch workwear with holes, tears, or patches. At our house, barbwire is the number one reason clothes get cursed, patched, turned into grease rags, or used for dog house bedding. Oftentimes when I am wearing clothes victimized by barbwire in public, strangers and sometimes friends will mistake me for a peasant.

> *"I'm not gonna say a bad word to you; I'm just gonna say it to myself."*
>
> *~Reneé age 3*

Clothing isn't even safe from a measly barb prick. A poke from a fence barb in the knee vicinity might not rip a hole in a pair of jeans but eventually threads will begin to unravel and widen the hole until it's big enough to get snagged again or tear under pressure and body movement.

I do, however, seem to fit in well with the younger crowd, and my daughter accepts me for not wearing "mom pants" but rather jeans with a few well-placed tears in my jeans. I've seen new denim jeans that looked like they'd been cranked through a cotton gin. I can easily achieve the same thing with less effort by carelessly crossing barbwire fences and opening gates a few times. Top fence wires usually don't create much margin for short-legged people to swing a leg over a fence, and for me to squat down in order to get through the middle fence wires is not only unattractive to watch but something I am rarely successful at achieving without one item of clothing getting hung up on the fence.

My biggest ranch-related fear has always been worrying about mutilating a brand new pair of unharmed denim jeans, a nice looking top, or my jacket by accident while helping do a daily chore that involves an encounter with barbwire. This happens often when my family and I are on our way to church or headed someplace where we're going to be gone all day.

The good thing is that the barbwire snagged look is gaining in popularity these days. Brand new peasant wear is really in right now. I've seen new jeans that look just like my barbwire ripped pants in the girl's and women's section at clothing stores. Yet I still get discouraged in maintaining decent looking jeans. Ninety-seven percent of my pants get barbwire damaged, but since I opt to be too lazy to change at times and continually take chances wearing my good jeans to do simple ranch work, the remaining 3% of my jeans get damaged by manure stains that escaped pre-treating before washing.

An untidy array of boots and bootjacks is a common sight at the Kirk home.
(*Photo by Amy Kirk*)

Bootism Disease

My family has a genetic disease called bootism. It's a rare disease that typically affects only ranch families, but knowing that other ranch families like ours all over the country have too many cowboy boots is reassuring.

The disease can infect a person at infancy, as it did with both of my kids, and is often ongoing into adulthood. A common place where bootism strikes is at a baby shower. Someone gives the newborn his or her first pair of cowboy boots. The moment a baby's feet are exposed to boots, they contract bootism disease.

Seeing ranch kids wearing this particular footwear as they grow becomes commonplace. Since kids outgrow clothes and footwear so fast, ranch families regularly exchange or pass on boots in order to get the most out of them. Bootism among kids can occur through direct contact from the hands of other ranch families just from handing a pair over or by handing down boxes or bags of clothing containing kids' cowboy boots. The condition has a tendency to spread, whether boots are actively worn or dormant. The inactive ones generally don't surface until a kid's feet are able to fit into them. Boots around our household lie dormant in places like a closet, the attic, the porch, or the rafters of the shop.

This disease is powerful because ranch families are unable to reject most free boots, regardless of whether the boots are the right size for any of their family members. All youth boots received eventually end up on a ranch kid's feet. If one family doesn't have someone who can wear them, then the boots either go dormant for a while or get passed on to a family who may have someone with eligible feet, fully expecting to get the boots back at a later time.

Grown-ups are affected by bootism disease because ranchers and ranch wives wear boots on a daily basis for chores, horseback riding, and special outings. A tough pair doesn't die off easily, making boots hard to purge. Once a ranch kid quits growing, boots start to accumulate.

The reasons why adult boots on ranches are hard to get rid of vary. A nice pair might only go with one outfit because of its unique color; they're "parts" boots for repairing currently worn boots; they're kept as keepsakes to show others how much abuse cowboy boots can take, are saved as a backup pair, or are a sentimental heirloom to the wearer. Even when a boot style becomes unpopular, the boots are kept in case the style makes a comeback. Other reasons boots are hung onto is that they become uncomfortable to wear only after a couple of hours, not immediately; somebody had good intentions of taking a pair in for repairs someday, or the owner was too embarrassed to admit buying such hideous-looking bad-impulse boots that he or she doesn't even want the garbage man to see them.

Sometimes there's only one thing wrong with a pair, which isn't enough to justify tossing because of the money that was spent on them: the sole or stitching came apart, they eat socks, or rub a blister, so they become reserved for special duties. My husband's old lace-up packers are only worn for water-related work in stock tanks, springs, well housings, and dams.

The reason a cure for bootism hasn't been pursued is because the disease doesn't interfere with one's ability to enjoy life. Boots aren't abandoned regardless of their flaws, which makes for a lot of happy soles.

The Makings of a Cattle Ranch

People un-ranched are led to believe through western movies that a herd of cows is what makes up a cattle ranch. It's time to clear up this misconception: cows on a ranch are solely there to absorb money and time.

Cows are mainly just landscape ornaments scattered out on an extremely large-scale yard known as a pasture, where you can't see all of the cows or the fence containing them. One of the most pertinent elements that make up a ranch is location. Most ranches are located in places distanced from civilization. Ranches are also where muddy or snow-drifted driveways are maintained by the families that live there.

"Me an' Dad are goin' to work—we can't be goofin' around."
~Myles age 5

In addition to being far from town, another factor that makes up a ranch is having to go to work in extreme weather conditions. In wintertime there's snow, freezing cold temperatures, high winds, wind chill, or combinations of these. In summer there's heat, humidity, high winds, and gully-washer rains or a combination. Weather conditions make the ranch work of ensuring feed, water, salt and mineral, and herd health challenging and of constant concern year-round.

Unlike superficial movie ranches, real ones have junk yards which contribute to the makeup of the ranch. A junk yard is an acre or two of land dedicated to years worth of old machinery, family cars, windmill parts, scrap metal, used lick tubs, stuff to burn, and other junk saved for the purpose of baffling future generations as to why.

"Me an' Dad got a lotta beeswax to do!"
~Myles age 7

Another typical fixture that makes up a ranch is youth helping out. In the summertime they can be seen working alongside parents in hay fields and driving machines costing as much as a Hummer, only four times the size, more practical, and not as ugly.

A true cow outfit has things on it that have been on the place from the get-go and are part of a ranch's composition: vintage fences, original buildings, antiquated machinery, and rough-looking pickups. The average ranch has a few distressed-looking outbuildings still standing. In some instances the original buildings may be leaning but are still used, or there may be a mix of old and new buildings: a big new barn or machinery shed and a little old house. One building that reflects an era might be an outhouse—a two-seater if it's a big outfit/ranch. Such fixtures are not common anywhere else.

In addition to old outbuildings, outhouses, junk yards, and barn cats with no names, there are other items common to ranches. They include used machinery, horses and/or four-wheelers, at least one dog, mineral feeders, feed bunks, salt blocks, lick tubs, stock tanks, bulk fuel tanks, one of every kind of trailer, and a passel of dirty, four-wheel drive vehicles—unless cows have licked the dirt off.

Another characteristic common among ranches is age. Since the majority of cow outfits were established in the 19th and 20th century, most ranches have a rustic look. This style may give a ranch's age away but it also gives these places their authentic, tough-looking appearance.

When first-time guests visit our ranch it's no wonder they say they're envious of us. Not everybody gets to enjoy the privacy of his or her own outhouse.

Go with an Easy Gate

Trying to reason with a difficult gate is like talking to a post. Every gate has a different personality and when I have to open or close a gate, I find myself talking to it.

I don't always talk nice to the gates either; many try my patience. I get along with some gates better than others, like the newer stack yard gate at home. It's an attractive, red panel that gets a lot of attention, is in good shape and very approachable, although it is into chains.

I have a harder time liking the old stack yard gate north of Pringle. It's stubborn, unreasonable, and not very pleasant to be around. It ripped my down coat sleeve once, so I called it a few names and we've not gotten along since. As with all the other gates, my husband gets along with this one just fine, but I doubt that gate and I will ever see eye to eye. It tries to intimidate me because it's taller than I am (to keep elk and deer out) and won't let me reach its latch simultaneously when I squeeze it tightly. I've never been able to shut it up without a fight. We tussle every time we see each other and I'm embarrassed to admit I've even gotten my kids involved in my scuffles with it.

I'm not very patient with complicated gates when it comes to figuring them out. I dislike dealing with the ones that have issues. Then there are the corral gates with appendages that don't work so well any more. After being involved in a bad livestock holding wreck, they need a welding surgeon.

The corral gates where we winter our bulls got all bent out of shape one year, and those tough-looking buggers ended up crippled and permanently bent up as a result of a bull challenging them. I tend to ignore their groans when they're pushed or pulled on. A couple of gates that have been around the barn too long are big, wooden, and heavy, but want to be useful. Due to their age and weight, they need assistance in getting lifted up in order to latch shut when being moved around, and everything about them sags, unlike, of course, their owners.

Most of the gates that accessorize hang around in the corrals. They have fancy latches that all work differently to open. Each one tests my patience in recalling the little tricks in how to operate them. Some are really fussy or temperamental when I mess with their latches, but I don't coddle them.

Sometimes we get new gates that have latches that, at first glance look like a brain teaser puzzle to figure out. After fiddling around with them for five minutes, I realize that I made figuring them out harder than it really was. The gates that refuse to budge in the wintertime just want to be left alone. They're content to stay put in tall, dead grasses until summer and don't care to be useful so I have to yank on them to get them to move.

Of all the gates I deal with, there is one that I don't complain about. It's rarely used, but it's my favorite: the gate my husband gets.

Always Look Over Your Shoulder

I'm guessing that Henry David Thoreau never put up hay because his quote, "Never look back unless you are planning to go that way," is advice that wouldn't cut it during haying season. You always look back—a lot.

If I don't look back while running haying equipment, I'll most likely end up with a problem that I will need to resolve before I can continue. Similarly, if too much time passes between looking back, there's a pretty good chance I'll find something wrong when I do turn around. Witnessing the effects of mechanical oversights created by others that require my husband to have to stop what he's doing to fix, has caused me to develop paranoia over mechanical problems that are beyond my gender's capabilities, and I haven't stopped looking over my shoulder since.

> *"It looks like a windrower...and hay inside there."* (Watching his baby sister Reneé chew green beans)
>
> ~Myles age 6

Fortunately, there's great insight in what one leaves behind. Oftentimes what's behind me foretells what's ahead. While I'm raking, if a wad of hay gets tightly-packed between the rake and the wheels it means I get to stop and take a break, stretch my legs, get a drink of water, and pee if I need to. My husband doesn't like having to stop and get out of his tractor to help me unplug the rake or windrower because doing so usually makes his hayfever flair up. His eyes get red from rubbing the fire out of them and he doesn't have a hankie big enough to clear his stuffed-up nasal passages once exposed to hay dust. Hay fever is nothing to sneeze at when we're trying to finish haying a field before an approaching thunderstorm hovers overhead.

While windrowing, I always look back to ensure that I'm leaving something behind, and hopefully it's a windrow. If there's no regurgitated hay laying on the ground behind the windrower it usually means I went through a thick area too fast in an effort to reach the edge of the field so I could take a potty break. Once the windrower's conditioner is plugged, I have to stop where I'm at, get out, unplug the machine, and hope that no drivers can see me behind the windrower using the hay field as a restroom facility. Cutting and pulling hay out of the bowels of the windrower is a loathsome job, but not nearly as much as other jobs such as unplugging our toilet.

When I windrow or rake I look over my shoulder more than I look ahead, which isn't always good because my steering tends to drift in the direction that my head is turned. This causes the uncut hay I use as a guide to look wavy, but my lines are more artistic-looking than the lame and boringly straight ones that farmers and ranchers like my husband prefer.

Most of the problems I encounter while windrowing or raking are behind me and are fairly easy to resolve if I spend the majority of my time looking over my shoulder. The rest of my problems can usually be sorted out from the tractor seat.

Operating the windrower requires a lot of multi-tasking so three-fourths of my time is spent looking back to see if the windrower's plugged up, any rocks are digging a ditch behind me, or if any strips of hay got missed due to a broken sickle section resulting from my inattentiveness. When I'm windrowing or raking there's a lot more going on behind me that I need to be watching for than there is ahead of me, which may explain why I never know whether I'm coming or going much of the time.

Lonesome Dove Logic

Whenever I want to enlighten my husband and kids, I use a little *Lonesome Dove* Logic to trigger their attention and diminish their immunity to the sound of my voice.

My scheme to get heard involves recalling lines from my favorite characters in the classic western I never tire of watching; *Lonesome Dove*. Copping lines from the movie piques my family's attention. I compiled my top picks of *Lonesome Dove* Logic for other women interested in trying out this attention-getting approach. Just remember, husbands like to use it too.

"I see the mornin' rush ain't started yet."—A perfect early morning line to wake-up slow, sleepy-headed kids for school when nobody's very chipper or to make my presence known when I return home without a grand welcoming.

"There was no *fun* in the deal." If my husband tries to rally up the family for a cow-related job that frequently goes bad, this reminds him that no matter how he candy-coats it, I'm not going to be convinced it'll be *fun*.

"It's a hard trip." This gets the point across in a nice way when my husband or I want to do errands alone. It implies by coming along, the passenger will get bored and impatient with the planned stops and special ones haven't been allotted for.

"Where ya off to, lookin' so pretty?" I tease my husband with this one when he's headed somewhere without me and wearing his good shirt, jeans, boots and hat. It's my way of saying he looks sharp.

"Now we're gonna suffer for the rest of our dang lives."—What I say out loud in order to keep a sense of humor when things backfire. One instance would be my guys' shop projects that fail during use. Another is while moving cows, the kids and I only hear snapping tree limbs and my husband's loud swearing in the woods nearby, due to cows headed in the wrong direction.

"We done et!" is satisfying to say when my kids have been told to come and eat and don't show up in time or after supper when they want to make something that messes up the kitchen.

> *"Oh, that's just an old war weapon." (243 hunting rifle)*
> *~Myles age 11*

"H*** no, I ain't alright!" is a response that lets the spectating spouse know when asking "you alright?" after stubbing a toe, hitting his or her head, getting run over or kicked by a cow, that he or she is not alright.

"Pour me a drink…arguin' with you always makes me thirsty." This is a fun way to convince my husband to grab me a beer even though we're not arguing or when I'm looking for a way to make apologies if I've been crabby. If we are arguing, citing this line always stirs a look, a laugh, and an end to bickering.

"I wish I could say." When I can't bring myself to lie about problems I encountered while feeding cows and know that explaining would just aggravate him.

"I don't believe I can remember,"—a hinting response that if he persists, I'll be forced to tell him and he'll wish he'd never asked.

"Let's go on and go if we're goin'!" My spouse uses this on me **A LOT** to imply impatience, when we need to be leaving and everybody's in the car waiting on me while I'm still getting ready.

"I tell you what. You ride on up to (where the work is)…build a little cabin, get a nice fire goin' in the fireplace, and me an' the kids will come on up." My classic "call your bluff" line when my rancher-husband tries to buffalo me into helping him over the same chore that ended in a big ol' fight the last time.

"I oughtta kick ya for givin' 'im all them ideas about (<u>fill in the blank</u>)"—for the people who suggest a project idea for my husband or kids that I have to live with when it's being built, creates frustration, or fails. I always say this to no one in particular on near misses with Santa Claus, the Easter Bunny and that dang Tooth Fairy.

"...it's depressin' to talk to you." Repeating this helps turn skepticism around in a humorous way, when I'm optimistic and my partner's skeptical and negative.

And my personal favorite: **"I'm givin' you a reason to go on another adventure, so you don't get *bored* bein' a rancher."** What I tell my rancher to encourage a change in his attitude when we have to go somewhere he's not thrilled about leaving home for.

You can see there's a *Lonesome Dove* quote to suit any situation for drawing attention and hundreds more are in the movie; you just have to pick a few and try them out. They work with our without the South Texas accent.

If you've seen *Lonesome Dove* before, it's always worth watching again. If not, seeing it at least once is the logical thing to do.

Living the Simple Life

Thinking that my household needed to be simplified, I read a book about simplistic living ideas. I was amazed to learn that I didn't need to buy the book. I could have written it myself. We live by the words of Thoreau to "Simplify, simplify, simplify." My family has been doing the majority of the book's suggestions for years, which proves that we are ahead of the all-consuming times.

Reneé: "I just love the olden days." Amy: "How come?" Reneé: "No laws, you get to stay home and make things, and when I was smaller." (Before she had to go to school)

– Reneé age 5

One of the book's suggestions was to consider a smaller home. Our small house has simplified problems such as company staying for an extended visit. Staying here is like camping; visitors have to rough it without conveniences such as television or privacy. There's no guest room with a door or private bathroom because guests sleep on our hide-a-bed couch or floor and we only have one bathroom. My simple spending plan has allowed us to offer company the same hide-a-bed couch in our living room that we've had for 17 years.

It may seem hard to believe today, but we've managed to get by without a garage, the space designated to store people's overflow from their houses. Without a garage, I've eliminated the need to waste money on things like excess holiday decorations that aren't out long enough to pay for themselves and that require storage for 330 days.

I was familiar with the book's idea of having a moratorium on spending except to buy groceries and personal items. I do it because our ranch responsibilities and the distance we live from big box stores don't make it convenient to get away for frequent shopping, which has led to coming up with creative solutions rather than with buying solutions; another suggestion in the book.

I keep meal planning simple too. The majority of our meals consist of beef we raised and had processed. I can choose from a variety of beef cuts readily available in our chest freezer. And cooking is simplified when I mix a bunch of ingredients together and let my crockpot do all the cooking, which eliminates dirtying several pots, pans, and utensils.

Evidently, eating meals together is another novel idea, which wasn't in the book. Nevertheless, I've overheard complicated moms talking about this problem when it is really a simple practice. I've simplified family meetings by using mealtimes to fulfill several family needs simultaneously. Mealtimes are the only opportunities we all sit down together without rearranging schedules to accommodate each other. It's the only time my kids volunteer information freely about their teachers and classes, daily activities, and classmates. Our family lives together, gathers together, converses together, and eats together by discussing each of our day's news while enjoying an evening meal around our kitchen table.

"Mom, I was hoping you could talk to me about my life." (worried)

~ Reneé age 5

Our family time is simple too. We spend it as family feeding cows, fixing fences, putting up hay, checking cows, or moving them to summer range. My simple parenting style includes eliminating busy time fillers that take them away from home so that our kids have an excuse to enjoy downtime at home and being kids. As a result, they're more self-sufficient. They can sufficiently entertain themselves by making up immature lyrics, silly rhymes, and strange noises, mocking me, or creating different ways to annoy me.

One way we live simply is to find ways to reuse what we already have. For generations, ranch families distanced from town have had to rely on the resources around them, improvise, and make do out of necessity. This concept may seem simple, but evidently the idea needed revisited because this gal was able to sell her book explaining how people

"This is making me domesticated." (hour-long car ride)

~ Myles 12

can reuse their old stuff in new ways. A lone hubcap makes a great barn cat dish, holey underwear suffices as a grease rag, and baling wire fixes and holds together almost everything (duct tape doesn't have the holding and lasting power that baling wire does).

I did find it surprising that filling the dishwasher and washing machine full before running them had to be suggested. I always considered those simple habits no-brainers, but water conservation has also been a longtime practice on ranches mostly out of necessity and is a widely used practice that continues today.

Some people may consider us "simple folk" based on our lifestyle, but we take it as a compliment. Books are written about the practices folks like us use.

Cowboy Logic Camping

In today's society, the concept of camping is to get away from civilization that's familiar and to experience the outdoors at a campground with strangers and enough sites next to each other to simulate a neighborhood-away-from-home.

When our kids mentioned how much they liked staying at a campground, my husband told them, "A campground is about as close to living in town as you can get." Many campgrounds are bustling with people and pets and are filled with campers and things that signify "roughing it," like full hookups, fire starter lighter fluid, street lights, cell service, vault toilets and satellite access. Since campgrounds are the only public places designated for campfires, my husband and I have gone against our camping morals and taken our kids to a campground for a couple of nights. Their idea of camping is solely to sit around a fire pit, stare at coals glowing in the dark, overdose on s'mores, then circle the fire pit repeatedly to dodge smoke getting in their eyes.

> *"Momma, when we go to the Big Horns, I wanna bring my harmonica." (on a trail riding and camping trip in the Big Horns)*
>
> *~Myles age 8*

Campground life takes some getting used to for our family. The nonstop traffic that laps the one-way drive through the campground makes I-90 through South Dakota seem like a seldom-used cow trail. I've felt safer blocking a hole from spooked heifers than I have watching out for campers looking for available campsites instead of the road. Having our space and privacy encroached upon by strangers occupying the surrounding campsites is hard to get used to. At home, the closest neighbor's place is a few hills over from ours. I'm a little creeped out when I can hear the people at the campsite next to ours passing gas and their topics of conversation. It violates my personal space's comfort zone. Dogs barking, people walking by watching us circle around our campfire and noisy four wheelers constantly going past us overloads our simple minds.

When our kids ask us if we can all go camping, their dad reminds them if they want to camp like the *cowboys* did, we've got the whole valley right at home to do that. Persuaded, our son would drag out his saddle, wool blanket, cowboy hat and boots to "camp" cowboy style in our backyard with his long johns on, just to get the full cowboy camping experience.

There are no strangers, campground lighting, or motorized racket makers around when we camp in our "valley." The only noises we hear are chirping crickets, croaking frogs, yipping coyotes and cow elk calling their young—all under a big sky for us to easily watch the stars come out since we don't have a sodium yard light. We eventually resolved the kids' penchant for a campfire by creating an outdoor fire pit.

My husband's words evidently stuck with our kids about camping at home. While gazing up at the stars one night from her sleeping bag, our young daughter said emphatically, "I just like campin' in our own *valley!*"

When our family gets curious about what it's like to live in a city, we stay at a crowded campground filled with complete strangers for a few days. We always come back home with a renewed appreciation for isolation.

South Dakota: The Hard Worker State

South Dakotans have a reputation for being hard workers. The fact that the state mammal is the coyote (a scavenger), and that every year the residents survive South Dakota's winters should be one's first clue.

South Dakotans come from a long line of hard-working people because it's necessary in order to survive living here. The pioneers who homesteaded our state were the first to discover that living in South Dakota would not be simple. Nothing they got was easily attained, be it food, winter heat or sanity. Settlers courageous enough to homestead on South Dakota's prairies had to work hard to endure the harsh winters. Laura Ingalls Wilder summed up South Dakota's longest season perfectly by naming a book after it: "The Long Winter." She depicted the stamina it took for her to survive the chore of grinding wheat in a coffee grinder and twisting hay all day and how Pa worked his britches off when the team got stuck in the slew.

> *"My knuckles have had a hard week!"*
> ~*Myles age 8*

For the people from the Mount Rushmore State, everything's harder, especially in the Black Hills. It's hard digging wherever a fence post needs to go because the soil is 85% rock. The 15% of dirt is on the surface. Even the water is hard in parts of South Dakota.

Our state is also a place that's hard to get out of. Just ask anyone who's ever been stuck in South Dakota's sticky gumbo mud. It's not every state where people have to dig out of snowdrifts or washed-out muddy roads before going to town unless they live in South Dakota. Still, residents are anxious to work especially since there really isn't much else to do when hunting season is over. And once winter is over, work is a desirable activity to many South Dakota residents—the weather is much warmer to work in and people don't have to wear three layers of clothing to work everyday.

A drawback to being a sparsely populated state is that there isn't the abundance of jobs compared to the more densely populated states. South Dakotans do what's necessary to make a living and that generally means work. Residents know that they have to bust their tails at their jobs or somebody else will to get it. But that's usually not a problem because South Dakotans are also an ambitious bunch. Few states like South Dakota have ancestors who built their homes out of dirt and grass known as a soddy or sod house. I don't know how else to prove that South Dakotans are hard workers other than to mention that our state has not one, but two, mountains that have been carved into monuments. You just don't find that kind of motivation in every state.

> *"I've been through a lot of disasters: stitches, I'm gonna have braces...."*
>
> *~Myles age 9*

A lot of the jobs that are available in South Dakota involve labor. Most of the land is used for agriculture, and fields don't plow, plant, or harvest themselves. Many South Dakotans get to work early. Legally, kids can get a job at 14 and a driver's license to get to work at 14, but many youngsters on farms and ranches start helping out at half that age. Farm and ranch kids are expected to help out at a young age, but many teens who live in town get jobs on farms or ranches also.

The only time South Dakotans have it easy is when they apply for jobs in other parts of the country. Employers who receive a South Dakotan's job application know the applicant can do the job because that application shows extensive experience in working hard.

Baling Wire: Saving Bales and Then Some

The secret to the success on our ranch besides a lot of work is baling wire. Between my husband and me, it takes a lot to hold a ranch together, mostly a lot of baling wire. We fix the majority of our problems with this ranch necessity.

We have an old Massey Ferguson square baler that's temperamental every time we use it, but it's always been a part of our ranch because its main purpose is to contribute to resolving all the rest of the ranch-related problems we have. This outdated haying equipment makes handy-sized lengths of reusable baling wire. Another neat feature is that it produces square hay bales. Wire-tied bales can be stored for years and mice can't chew the wire like they can the twine version.

Baling wire is so durable that a little scrap goes a long way, especially when there's a lot of it on hand. We tuck it between barn walls, twist it on onto portable panels, gates, and fences, hang it off four-wheelers, and stow it behind pickup seats for added convenience and availability.

Money, tools, and replacement parts also go a lot further because they aren't always necessary. As long as we have some "miracle wire" on hand, we can fix just about anything. Serious ranch related headaches like broken fence wires, tractor hood latches or other parts that vibrate loose, and livestock tank floats that get knocked around, usually get repaired with baling wire in some way.

A rancher can't go wrong with baling wire because it doesn't take up much space, is cost-effective, and comes off the bale in a handy length. It's usually enough to do the job and is readily available for fixing a problem.

Besides being the easiest ranch staple to work with, it serves a multitude of uses. Baling wire suffices to repair headstalls and bicycle parts, make key rings, car antennas, hooks, or replacement handles on five gallon buckets. It'll hang Christmas ornaments and outdoor lights, and replaces fence clips, hose clamps, gate chains, and door latches. It secures broken fence wires, holds livestock panels together, and will keep a car's headlight in place as well as a car battery, but baling wire isn't just for fixing problems. It makes dandy marshmallow skewers, stringers for fishing; hangers for flower baskets and birdhouses, and makes wire-rimmed glasses for a Granny Clampett Halloween costume. Even rusty baling wire serves as a reliable fix on machinery, vehicles, or fences until it can be properly replaced with a new piece of baling wire.

Old timers know leftover baling wire is the most versatile, inexpensive and valuable resource in ranch country. Many have asked us if they could have some of ours when they spot it wrapped on our pickup's headache rack. My husband's even been asked for a feed sack's fill by other ranchers who know the value of the good, multi-purpose material.

Like others who are familiar with and highly dependent on this wire, we can't live without it. Miracle wire is tough, reliable, and adaptable to most tasks, it's long-standing and generally always on hand. Its strength and durability holds up well under all kinds of circumstances yet is easy to work with due to its flexibility. Basically, baling wire is like having a ranch wife around.

Eyesore, My Eye!

I can't imagine life without a clothesline, but evidently some people can't imagine life with one. I wrongly assumed once that everybody has experienced line-dried clothes and loves the smell of fresh air in their laundry as I do.

When I pluck sun-dried laundry off the line, I like to inhale the fresh scent no fabric softener can duplicate. On windy days or nights, I enjoy the sound of laundry flapping in the breeze. Those breezes snap wrinkles right out of shirts, jeans and sheets and Mother Nature starches them for me too.

I was asked once what the point of drying clothes outside was. I explained the advantages of saving electricity and asked my clothesline-deprived guest if these great inventions were used where he lived. That's when I learned that not everyone enjoys seeing other people's laundry hanging outside and that clotheslines are considered an eyesore in some places.

Rows of laundry waving in the wind are the last thing I would have considered a landscape blemish. The surprising comment just proved to me that where people live determines what they consider ugly in other parts of the country. Some of the biggest eyesores I've ever seen are sun-bleached white trash bags hung up on fences that flutter in the wind and trees that nobody is eager to go up and touch, smell, and take down.

I consider most urban environments an eyesore. From a distance while driving at night, I notice a radioactive orange glow coming from the overkill of blazing orange street lights. The type of wash left outside to dry in many cities are piles of fast-food cups, plastic lids, straws, and food packaging banked against street curbs and drains.

I'm grateful for my clothes dryer in the wintertime, but whenever I get summer withdrawals, my remedy is to hang loads of washed laundry on my clothesline. Once warmer days arrive, I ditch my dryer for the starchy feel and wonderfully fresh scent of line-dried laundry. Towels, shirts, and linens suck up all the fresh air they can hold while waving up and down in the wind. The distinctive scent clings to my sheets, lulling me to sleep, sweetening my dreams, and temporarily satisfying my cravings for hot summer days.

Maybe metropolitan people are more modest about hanging their underwear where people can see them, but I'd still rather hurt my eyes looking at somebody's clean and bright tighty-whitey underwear or bras strung out on a line than people's dirty white trash hung up in trees and fences. I could relate to people who think line-dried laundry is an eyesore if their problem with clothes drying

How could anyone not love the sight of clothes on a clothesline especially when it's a clothesline like this one? I think I've done my job here--little Reneé putting "clothes" on her clothesline just like she's seen me do hundreds of times. Seeing clothes on the line is one of my favorite country views and perks to country life.

(*Photo by Amy Kirk*)

outside was in regards to the extra time it takes just to get laundry on and off the clothesline. Whenever I recruit my family to help with handling clean, wet clothes in strong winds or getting dried laundry off the clothesline before it rains or strong winds blow it away, my family always hangs me out to dry.

Plans That Fly

You can't get anywhere without an education these days, and my husband and I get one every time we count on our plans to fly accordingly when we're doing ranch work involving cows.

The most important lesson to know about making plans regarding livestock is that they are likely to get changed, especially when cows take off on a dead run ahead of us, so we need to be prepared to have to wing it at some point.

Winging it is the end result of the process of elimination. The weather will eliminate the use of certain corrals and loading areas when they get muddy. Cows will eliminate cooperation when we need them to. Sometimes when my spouse and I work together it eliminates our patience with each other and our tempers eliminate caring what the other thinks. These are all reasons why we don't put all our faith into one plan.

> Amy: *"Why aren't you eating leftovers?"*
> Myles: *"Cuz we gotta eat on the fly."*
> -Myles age 7

In planning, it helps to know that anything can happen when dealing with unpredictable things like tempers. Cows are predictable in that they'll frequently do something we weren't expecting. It's also wise to become familiar with all of the worst-case scenarios, which happen easily for us. In the back of my mind I expect the worst because that's where a lot of our plan A's have ended up. We can't outguess what a cow will do every time, but past cattle-related experiences have given us a pretty good idea of what kind of shenanigans cows will try.

We also know that having alternative strategies is good insurance against our superstitions coming true. We commonly have run-ins with Murphy's Law if we don't come up with a backup plan or two. Without one, we end up with a disaster on our hands that creates a no-plan approach of "winging it." We've become superstitious because when we wrongly assume a job will be easy to carry out or won't take very long and we didn't come up with a backup plan, something usually goes awry. Yearlings won't load in the trailer easily, it's too muddy to back the trailer up to the best loading spot, cows call our bluff to lure them into corrals, or we ignore an important element in carrying out our day's main mission—having enough manpower.

Plan A usually involves some willing cows, more than two adults, good weather, and good moods—a near-impossible combination and the reason why we have come to expect the likelihood of incorporating plan B. Plan B is essentially full coverage insurance—it rarely pays to have it. It's when my husband and I are short on livestock panels, patience, and manpower, or we expected our kids to be equally effective as adults helping us and it's too late to change our minds. Plan C is your typical liability coverage: it doesn't do much for *you* once there's a wreck. At this stage, frustrations are near-peaked from a situation's chaos.

The ability to accomplish something on short notice is also important in ranch work. It pertains to hurrying, unavailable help (kids), sudden or unexpected changes in plans, unforeseen circumstances, and unaccommodating weather forecasts for the day we chose to carry out our mission. Executing these short-notice chaotic ways of getting a big job done involving livestock is called winging it and we've gotten good at it. Winging it is doing ranch work that's not thought out very well or at all and is accomplished by instinctive reactions. We are most successful at winging it which is something that's just not heard of much with plan A mainly because with winging it, we expect everything to go wrong.

Winging it is the easiest plan to master because there's no strategizing. When we decide to do something last minute, have another engagement on the same day, or figure on doing the work shorthanded in a timely manner, the cows usually take care of the rest.

Manipulating My Family with Colorful Clothes

I enjoy messing with my family's minds and recently discovered a new way to do it. According to an article I read in a women's magazine, I can influence their moods with the color of my clothes.

The idea of wearing specific colors to get a certain reaction out of the people I'm around is appealing to me since my family seems immune to my voice. I may be on to something by letting the color of my clothes do my manipulating. This new approach could radically change the tone of workplace morale around here.

For instance, come sale day I plan on wearing something blue. Selling our calf crop is an important day and usually stress-filled. There's stress over having enough help to gather the herd, getting cows into the corrals, getting all of the sorts done before the truck arrives, loading the calves and trucking them to the sale barn, and then watching them sell. A year's worth of intense hard work for 365 days straight with no day off is quickly evaluated and its monetary value is determined. In less than five minutes our annual income is determined by an auction bid on our calf crop. It's just a little stressful on sale day. What my spouse needs on the day we sell our calf crop is serenity, which supposedly can be achieved if I wear soothing and calming blue-colored clothing.

Green is another good color choice and simple enough for me to incorporate since manure is abundant and is the color of our boots and clothes at times. This color is associated with nature (no-brainer there) and suggests peace and contentment; both ideal mood-enhancing colors for my family. Another mood I like to encourage that green is said to invoke is happiness. This explains why so many people are happy on Saint Patrick's Day. It's all the green beer they drink.

Black is the signature color of authority, which explains why it suits my husband because the wearer is viewed as being very capable. When I want to dismiss people's doubts about my abilities or confirm what I'm made of, I'll put something black on. It also conveys high quality; something I always strive for in my work unless I'm dealing with pre-existing crappy fences.

When our kids aren't overjoyed about a family day of ranch work and they need a mood booster, the best color for me to wear is something orange. It's considered an enthusiastic color. Even though I'm enthusiastic by nature, my family doesn't always share my energetic, enthusiastic mood. With a splash of orange, I can make them all feel like we're going to have some fun! Plus they'll be able to spot me anywhere easily.

If I want my husband to chase after me instead of our cows, I'll throw on something red. Red is the color of romance. As long as I've brushed my teeth and showered, wearing red could be the perfect way to redirect his attention. Since most of our together-time is spent around cows and date nights are few, wearing red when we're working together could make ranch work seem lovely.

My favorite color, purple, inspires creativity. I consider myself a creative person, but wearing purple could help my husband out when we have to be creative in resolving ranch-related problems. Purple also conveys independence which I possess. That doesn't mean diddly to a cow, but I like expressing it toward my family now and then.

Now I have a new purpose in picking out my clothes every morning. I choose my wardrobe according to the kind of moods I want to deal with.

The True Meaning of Fall

The time is upon us. The air at dawn feels brisk. Foliage on trees begins to change color, and there's a thin layer of ice in our dog's water dish. Don't you just love fall? I don't.

Over the last several years these seasonal changes have come to mean one thing: fall dread. The type of dread in which I wake up wondering, "What kind of mayhem is awaiting me today?"

My husband and I split cow checking duties, and I usually tend to the replacement heifers' stock tank unless he has other tasks to deal with and needs me to check the range also. Checking cows on our Forest Service permit involves making a big loop to ensure stock tanks are filling up properly, salt is plentiful, and to note the whereabouts of our cows.

Depending on where I find them, I may not get home before lunch, so it's important that I eat a hearty breakfast. I've missed my all-important mid-morning snack time before and felt energetically diminished due to handling a time-consuming seasonal cattle crisis instead of snacking.

I have also learned to brace myself for finding morning cow-quandaries in the fall. I head out on high alert for misplaced "Monday Morning Specials." All that means is I look for signs that indicate herd-related problems normally reserved for Mondays—when I'm not fully conscious yet and get sandbagged with herd trouble. I always keep an eye out for signs on the gravel road indicating potential livestock issues ahead. These sources of anxiety would be cow pie splatterings on roads where cows aren't supposed to be.

Another contribution to fall dread is finding gates left open. This may appall you, but every year there is at least one hunter who does not know about gate-closing etiquette and will leave a gate open that was shut.

Previous fall stress has taught me that autumn mornings arrive heavy with anxiety. Therefore, it is not the time of year for scheduling appointments, making plans to attend meetings, or expressing my availability in the mornings. I've learned to block off September and October mornings for potential setbacks as part of my daily routine. Anytime I make plans before 1 p.m. Murphy's Law lets me know I'm not in charge of my own time.

Regardless how much forage is still available, at the drop of the mercury, cows think it's time to go home since we move them north of Pringle around this time. Every fall our cows forget that my husband is the micromanager of this outfit and has the say-so when it's time to head home.

When frost starts showing up, cows try to sneak home early. In the weeks prior to moving our herd home, it becomes a daily routine to look for a cow clique trapped at a corner fence unable to access water or AWOL cows trying to leave the range early. In severe cases of homesickness, they'll find holes or weak fences to push through and head in a northeasterly direction toward home. The lead cows and their groupies always try to trail themselves home on their own. By early October pushing stray cows back onto the permit becomes a near-daily routine.

As you can see, the events that occur here in the fall cause me to associate autumn with dread; I hate missing my snack time.

Cow Disclaimers

Friendly bantering between my husband and me over what's his, mine, and ours is part of our relationship. We especially like joking with each other about the cows we run and whom they really belong to.

Whenever my husband starts discussing upcoming work with cows, I ask jokingly, "Are we talking about *your* cows or *our* cows?" It's been a long-standing joke that when ranch work needs the whole family's cooperation, my husband will tell the kids and me, "We're a team," and everybody needs to help take care of "our cows." But the kids and I know he calls them "his cows" whenever we're not around and doesn't need help with them.

He does refer to the herd as "our cows," since he and I tend to them jointly, but the work each of us does is not fifty-fifty by any means. He spends more time around cows and feels more of an attachment to them than I do. If he feels too overloaded with information or lined out with too many chores that aren't cow-related, he'll remind me that he needs to be checking on "his cows." Laundry, cooking, and supervising kid chores or homework, are all tasks he'll oversee in a pinch, but he likes it better when I'm in charge of those chores so he can go check cows.

I don't mind calling them our cows as long as herd problems are controllable, but if they are being difficult and make me mad, I call them "his cows." It might be a big cow dilemma that's difficult for me to handle alone, or having a solution to a cow problem backfire on me. Whatever the case may be, I'm usually too indecisive in solving cow troubles by myself and get stressed over trying to figure out what Art would do. He does a much better job at getting the floats on water tanks to work, catching a calf in the open, or doctoring livestock out on the range when he's alone. I'm always relieved when he can take over difficult challenges, just like he's glad when I'm available to manage our kids' appointments, practices, 4-H meetings, and parent volunteering.

When cows are manageable, the work goes smoother, but occasionally trouble shows up. Unexpected problems cause stress, frustration, and tension between my husband and me. We try to work together as a team, but depending on the severity of the circumstance, sometimes that theory gets booted. Each of us does whatever we feel is necessary to regain control when we run into problems, like cows heading in the wrong direction while trailing them home or calves that won't go through a gate. He and I react differently, and sometimes we end up bickering about the situation regarding "his cows;" at which point I'm in total agreement with, and don't contest.

Occasionally, my husband will disclaim cows too, when somebody tells him we have cows out and he has to go to take care of them. He's more than happy to call problem cows "somebody else's cows" if it turns out that they were the neighbors' or another ranch's range cows.

The Kirk Ranch's Problem-Solving Flow Chart

Resolving most problems around here entails a process of elimination, namely my affiliation with it, but sometimes different resolutions may have to be tried.

After years of observing my husband and father-in-law work together, I've figured out the Kirk ranch's problem-solving techniques. If you suffer from a lot of unresolved problems, you may want to adopt their techniques. It's a very straight-forward process to implement that's easy to figure out in a short period of time.

Oftentimes problems can be eliminated simply by assessing who is nearby who might have the slightest bit of information to help you resolve the problem. Your best sources will most likely be loved ones. Beginning at the top of the problem-solving flowchart, you should nonchalantly look around and ask yourself a simple question: "Who here can be blamed for the problem I've encountered?" It may take some creative thinking as to how you can twist the situation around so that someone else can be blamed, thus forcing him or her to deal with the problem so you can move on until you find yourself faced with another one.

"If you're thinkin' it was me, it was." (left a mess)

– Reneé age 4

"I didn't see myself do it."

– Myles age 5

If no one is around, think of someone, maybe the last person whom you saw where the problem occurred who could take the fall. If no one comes to mind, do some backtracking and think harder before you resort to looking in a mirror.

If you encountered some resistance and the problem still exists, you'll have to move on. This is where you may need to cowboy or cowgirl up and face your fears: reality. It may not have occurred to you before but if you don't come up with someone you can blame and who is gullible enough to accept it, the next step is to consider whether or not you can you fix the problem yourself. If it's possible, then ask yourself, "Does it need to be held together?" If yes, move ahead.

Assess the situation and determine first if baling wire can fix it and most importantly, do you have some behind the pickup seat? This can fix a multitude of recurring or newly developed problems. Many times this temporary fix will suffice at least until you die, as your children, once grown can attest to.

If baling wire isn't available, do you remember which pickup you last saw some duct tape rolling around in? It's world-famous for its fix-it capabilities. If you answered "yes," then estimate how much you will need to render the problem repaired. If baling wire and duct tape are absent from your floorboards, black electrical tape oftentimes kept in a glovebox has been proven to make a fine problem-solving substitute.

> "Don't ya know what whinin' is?"
>
> ~Reneé age 6

If your problem doesn't need held together or it still exists, your next question is, "Do you need to outsource the work to fix it?" Essentially, is there someone you could collect a favor on?

Note that hiring a professional is not mentioned as an alternative. The fact is that professionals fix things according to so-called "code," they charge you for it, and your frequent complaints about the expense will annoy at least one family member per household.

If any of these techniques don't work for you, don't blame me. I'm just passing on what I've learned.

Redneck Bragging

Dropping hints or buying items to boast one's financial status isn't a cattleman's style. We ranching folk aren't immune to showing off, we just do it in a "keeping-up-with-the-Foxworthy's" sort of way.

We prefer letting what seems legitimate brag for itself: cows, equipment, hay, and work crew; all of which ideally either contribute in a round-about way to making money or saving money, but cows and equipment usually only contribute to breaking even. We don't make out like we're better than anybody else regarding our social status either, just that we're money-smarter, common sense-wiser, and problem solving-handier.

> "Those guys are modest." (Clampett's on The Beverly Hillbillies)
>
> ~Myles age 12

We'll talk about our money too. We'll tell others how much money we would never be willing to spend, how much we didn't spend, or how much we saved by buying used or off brands.

We don't own vehicles that don't do anything other than decorate a driveway for status symbol purposes or try to increase others envy with. Instead we have several *old* outfits that fill up the driveway and all serve a functional, work-related purpose: feeding livestock, making hay to feed livestock, hauling livestock or their water; it's usually all about the cattle.

Ranchers will spend a lot of money on "wheels" too, but they provide the kind of ride that is really big, has four-wheel drive, drives in all sorts of weather and most field conditions, handles jobs it wasn't designed for, and helps to earn an income. Everybody notices our "wheels" because ours are three times the size of an Escalade, take up the road, and everybody has to slow down and give us a wide berth when we drive down the highway. We also boast on vehicles with 200,000 miles that aren't showing any signs of wearing out any further (translated: not running).

My husband likes to crow about how his pickups have never been washed and are still rust-free—as near as he can tell. He's also got one-of-a-kind outfits that have earned special bragging rights. We own vehicles and ATVs that have survived welding alterations and additions to accommodate every ranch season and ranch job including an SUV converted into a pickup, a bale roller bumper for a Toyota pickup also equipped with a winch that winches 2,000 pounds, and ATVs with welded on accessories to pack coffee mugs, calves, fencing materials, sorting sticks, and spotlights. Our haying equipment is classic too. Most of our equipment has parts that have to be *special ordered.*

Many ranchers like my husband have equipment to put up hay and like to let the sight of their haying operation do the bragging for them. Having a field dotted with hay bales that have been baled at the perfect time and are nice-looking round bales, massive amounts of hay, and horse-lover people stopping us while picking up small-sized square bales in the ditch and wanting—sometimes pleading—to buy our hay is all brag-worthy.

Cattlemen, my husband included, won't come out and brag about it, but they like being reputed for having impressive looking and behaving livestock that draws compliments. Mild-mannered bulls, replacement heifers that calve with ease their first time and have good motherly instincts, 600-700 pound calves on sale day, and healthy, young, nice-looking Marilyn Monroe-ish cows with a BCS (Body Condition Score) score of 6-7, not the Angelina Jolie cows scoring 1 or lower, are all brag-worthy.

When a rancher's kids reach maturity and can handle responsibility of an adult (for some ranch kids it's 12, for others it's 10) the ranchers like to boast about their kids helping in the hay field, being able to throw bales, or holding a calf down without it getting away to be branded or doctored on. It's an ego stroke when a rancher's children are highly sought after at branding time for the kids' ability to hustle, be respectful of others' property and livestock, work hard, and yet still act semi-domesticated away from home. Ranchers have trophy wives too and like to let their wives do the showing off. You know the kind, a woman who can back up a gooseneck trailer to a chute like a truck driver, run all the different equipment, cook for the 20-40 people helping at their branding, and can save a calf when her husband has his doubts.

A rancher brags about all of these things until they frustrate him or try his patience. Then he'll demonstrate a special behavior that isn't worth bragging about.

Just Leave Me in the Dark

I'm left in the dark at our place a lot but it doesn't bother me. I'm comfortable in the dark.

Once my husband and I moved into the home where we live now, I insisted that the sodium yard light that came on automatically every night had to go. I couldn't get used to its sharp light shining through our windows like a car's high beams, and it irked me that I couldn't manually shut it off.

I didn't like our yard being lit up all night with harsh fluorescent light casting its rays everywhere. I realized that I preferred instead, the warm, soft, yellow glow from those energy-sucking light bulbs that use a switch to turn them on and off. The amount of money or energy that sodium yard lights saved didn't compare to the savings of sleep from not having one on at all, so my husband appeased me and had the yard light taken down.

I don't consider it a bad thing that our place goes unnoticed at night either. I couldn't run out to a vehicle or gather clothes off the line in my skivvies at night if there was a yard light on and cars driving by. The absence of light doesn't announce to passersby where we live, and as far as the security that a yard light provides, our dog does a better job than any yard light.

I know a yard light gives some people peace of mind when they're sleeping, but yard lights aren't soothing or calming to me at all. Their annoying presence wakes me up or keeps me awake and makes me feel too restless to fall back asleep easily. If our yard needs lighting for expectant guests or to investigate a noise or activity outside, the porch light does the job just fine and I can shut it off once lighting is not needed.

I don't regret getting rid of our yard light. They ruin the dark, star-studded nights that I prefer, and yard lights don't provide the same soothing and calming ambiance that full moons do. Summertime campouts in our backyard wouldn't be the same with a yard light shining in our eyes and blocking the view of the super stars that we look up to. Yard lights can't compare to the shooting stars that brighten our family's nights while drifting off to sleep.

Being in the dark to enjoy the Milky Way, meteor showers, and full moons is all I need to light up my life. Sodium yard lights just turn me off.

Our Eight Minutes of Fame

Technically, it was only 7:47 minutes. It was originally two days worth of filming, but the idea was to keep viewers interested.

The day that Erika Kotite of Kotite Media Group contacted me about the possibility of filming the process of putting together our branding day dinner, I assumed it was going to be a documentary about rural chaos. She had a video series called *What's For Dinner America?* on her *Toque Magazine* cooking website that featured how different cooks put dinner on the table in unique ways.

> *"Reneé should be on a cooking show."*
> *~Myles age 10*

She and I had known each other for a while, and oftentimes I would tell her about the fun job I was currently doing on our ranch: dealing with cows that got out, calving problems, water troubles, or fence fixing. One time I talked about an upcoming branding that I was preparing dinner for. I explained that I try to make it easy on myself on branding day and do most of my stressing out in the kitchen beforehand so I can be a part of the branding at the corrals. This all fascinated her, and she thought this kind of gathering for food would make an interesting episode for her video series.

The goal was to show viewers what was involved to prepare and feed the 20-40 people who help us brand every spring. Erika's videographer taped 48 hours of the annual event bedlam inside and outside of my kitchen.

> *"Go see if supper's not cooked right."*
> *(timer went off and he wanted to play longer)*
> *~Myles age 8*

Erika and the videographer wanted to depict a typical western South Dakota springtime branding, and May 1st was our branding day. The weather helped us out immensely. We had nearly every kind of weather condition before noon. The whole day illustrated perfectly why South Dakota is less populated than other states.

Branding that day was like being inside a snow globe. It was cold, and strong erratic winds pushed everybody around. We had quick-changing cloud cover, periodic bouts of snow that looked shaken up instead of fallen, and cows bunched up in different corners to escape the wind's constantly changing direction. The video captured the western-style mayhem we dealt with on that branding day flawlessly. Once branding and the dinner was over, the winds died down and the sun came out, belatedly perfect for a branding.

Describing what I did to prepare for the meal made me sound like I was an efficient, multi-tasking cook able to put on such a big feed and still be a part of the branding work outside.

I think I was successful in fooling viewers with my tidy kitchen habits and portraying myself as an organized cook. Five-eighths of the filming done in the kitchen made for good footage to edit out. All the scattered clutter, messes, spills, array of ingredients, food scraps, and dinnerware, was hardly noticed in the final cut. There was enough footage for another video called "Documentary of a Slob in The Kitchen."

Overall, being filmed was an enjoyable experience. Of all the things I learned about being on camera, I understand now why some Hollywood stars don't like watching themselves on-screen. Actresses look heavier on screen when they wear long johns.

Cows' Sixth Sense

Getting our cows home is always an adventure, but the one time we tried to move them to the grassier pastures of home we made the mistake of cavalierly believing the job would be relatively easy to pull off.

It should be noted that in dealing with animals, the chances of plan A and sometimes plan B being successful are about as likely as Britney Spears finding stability, contentment, or a marriage that will last. Even though we achieved our goal of getting our cows home that day (we weren't considering any other option), the successes are never remembered as much as the challenges. No matter how much planning ahead we do, we always figure on some degree of improvising.

> Art: "My patience is runnin' short!"
> Reneé: "That means mad."
> ~ Reneé age 4

Within a half an hour, the start of our day's work felt like the foretelling of a disaster of great magnitude. Our cows applied their seldom-used sixth sense: that of detecting trickery. They sensed they were being tricked into believing they were getting fed, which they actually were, but only after we got them in the corrals first. They're trained to come to feed to the sound of a short series of honks on our pickup's horn and will do so except in instances when they sense our desperation in needing them to cooperate with us.

The herd began to trail toward the sound of the pickup's horn to the bale bed pickup like normal with the exception of a small bunch of cows that didn't want to follow at all. Once we positioned the feed pickup on the other side of the underpass so they could see the bale loaded on the pickup in our attempt to lure them through the underpass, they balked at our bluff to get them to go through. Getting cows to trail through the underpass is never a problem until it's mandatory. This time it was necessary in order to get them transported home where a pasture of fresh grass was waiting for them.

They also sensed our foolishness in expecting our plan to work and took advantage of the opportunity to be difficult. In instances such as these we learn so much from our cows, like how not to be overconfident in expecting a plan to go accordingly. Even more, we were reminded of the all important role of winging it.

We overestimated their motivation to follow the feed pickup and underestimated the need for extra horses, four-wheelers and riders to gather. When the herd reached the underpass they bunched up and stood in front of it. Their deadpan expressions while standing stock-still revealed a sense of amusement at our efforts to get them to go through the underpass. They watched our various attempts at maintaining our bluff in order to get them to the corrals to be loaded and hauled home. It wasn't until our crew put enough pressure on them by crowding up on them from behind them and next to them that they became convinced that they weren't going any other direction but forward and they eventually moved ahead. Getting the small bunch that wouldn't follow the pickup to the corrals proved to be a sub-challenge. The cows weren't in the mood to cooperate. We had to constantly make adjustments in our plan to get them through the underpass to the other side where we could gather them in the corrals and load them into stock trailers using the loading chute, and haul them to their winter pasture.

Being persistent, determined, and passionate about achieving our goal is how we get things done and is the reason why the cows finally went through the underpass. In the end, the job was considered a success, mostly because we didn't consider any other option—the cows were going to get moved home, and there was minimal tension, but most importantly, the day didn't end up a disaster of Britney Spears magnitude.

Art and the kids enjoying the view of Pringle and reading names carved on the car for a family day hike up to the Pringle Poacher Car on Kirk property fifteen years after the car's placement on the rock ledge. We concluded our hike with a summer evening picnic watching the sun set. (*Photo by Amy Kirk*)

Pringle's PPA (Pringle Poachers Association) Monument

Our southern Black Hills hometown of Pringle, which is out-populated by the area's elk, knows how to laugh in the face of adversity. The proof is at the top of the hill and overlooks the town.

The community's unofficial monument isn't obvious, well advertised, or the most photo-worthy site in the Black Hills, nor is it a popular tourist destination, but any local loves to point it out.

As one looks west toward the rocky ridge from downtown Pringle, the monument sits broadside on a steep rock face. Once a contrasting blue that stood out against the green pines and outcroppings of granite, the Pringle Poacher car is now so sun-faded it's camouflaged. Without knowing what's behind the hill by the car's location, one might think it had to have been airlifted there. Only locally grown Pringle Boys could have gotten it there any other way.

Like Mount Rushmore, it isn't supposed to be accessible to visitors, due to being on private property (ours), but initials and dates etched in the metal and stolen parts and emblems taken as tokens of the infamous car prove otherwise.

In the past, where the perpetration has stayed, an incident of poaching took place in the Pringle area. Several years later, a handful of young men (including my husband before we met) with an eccentric sense of humor took advantage of the mishap. The illegal activity branded Pringle as misfits by surrounding tourist-promoting towns and pompous hunters. The Pringle Boys founded the PPA (Pringle Poacher Association)—a tongue-in-cheek, informal organization of locals. The twenty-odd charter members, so-to-speak, called themselves the Pringle Poachers to keep people guessing as to the seriousness of the association. Business cards, T-shirts, and caps were made for publicity purposes at parades and community events. One of the members decided the PPA needed a Poacher car, which my husband proudly provided. He turned a 1969 Dodge Polara into a convertible by cutting the top off. It was decked out with steer horns at first, then elk horns, spot lights, a fake .50 caliber gun and the words "PRINGLE POACHERS" painted neatly in white boldface across the side door panels.

After the car died, memorializing the first Poacher car was my (still-single at the time) husband's brainchild. The hilltop was easier to access from his property on the backside of the ridge, and the insanely daring Pringle Poachers formulated a plan to pull the car to the top. It was a monumental job that took all day, using an old logging road, a log skidder, Pringle Boy testosterone-driven ambition, and the most essential component of any Pringle Boys' plan—Budweiser.

Three-fourths of the way to the top, progress halted due to the nearly vertical and mostly rocky slope. Hesitation and doubt regarding the risk seeped into the plan, forcing the crew back to the Hitchrail Bar and Restaurant for more beer-induced strategizing. Overhearing the discussion, another logger offered to give it a shot. The fearless skidder operator dragged the car up the remainder of the hill a little at a time then nudged it to the edge of the cliff, where it's become part of Pringle's horizon.

Pringle Poacher cars have been a part of the PPA's existence ever since. It may seem ludicrous that the group even exists, let alone is commemorated, but the Pringle Poachers proved that you should consider whom you look down on or you may find yourself looking up at their monument.

The welcome sign that greets motorists and visitors to our town: Pringle, South Dakota. Pringle's claim to fame is the elk population in our area. Oftentimes the elk population outnumbers the residents (population 125). (*Photo by Amy Kirk*)

Sleepless in September

September has arrived in the Black Hills. The morning air has gathered up a sharp edge, frost has been knocking on our windows, and leaves are being forced to change. My husband and I know what's coming next—insomnia.

Amy: "Did you have a good nap?" Reneé: "But I wanted to open my eyes."

~Reneé age 4

For much of September, I get shorted on sleep due to bull elk bugling every night until the eve of the opening day of elk hunting when all bugling ceases and the bulls disappear. During the rut, bull elk are saturated with testosterone as well as with urine. They wet themselves and raise a big stink over a bunch of female cow elk, but they also do it to distinguish themselves and their territory from other bulls. There's no mistaking bull elk. They have a distinctive smell—pungent. They also make equally distinctive racket.

The way bull elk communicate sounds a lot like normal downtown city noise. The sound a bull elk makes is similar to a hearing test. In one breath their bellows fluctuate from a deep-throated, raspy-hollow grunt, to a high-pitched echo-ey screech. The grunts remind me of when our son was little and growled into a vacuum extension hose. He was scared of the gravelly tone of his own voice so much that it took his breath away—the vacuum was on.

Throughout the month of September, bulls have nightly bugle-offs right outside our home. The loudest, most threatening and obnoxious bulls vie for cow elk like casino players gathering up poker chips. An annual bugle-athon takes place in our valley, and listening to them carry on is amazing. Bulls can bugle all night long, night after night, and never lose their voices.

One bleary-eyed September, we listened to two bulls flinging hefty insults back and forth from their domains, AKA our hay field. One bull was two hundred yards from our house and the other was down the valley half a mile. Both were full of bull—all bugling and no head-butting. Every night before bed, my husband and I could hear them threatening and belittling each other.

> *"I was having the finest sleep I ever had."*
>
> ~ Reneé age 6

Here's a translation of what we heard:

Old bull: "Why don't you go back to Wind Cave National Park and grow some real horns!"

Young bull: "You're so old you don't even have any ivory teeth left!"

Old bull: "You think you can get cows with *those* horns? You'll always be just a satellite bull, you dink rag horn!"

Young bull: "You couldn't even bring coyotes in!"

Old bull: "Well, you bugle like a *COW!*"

Young bull: "I don't think you even *HAVE* any cows up there!"

Old bull: "Is that the best you can bugle? All you can do for a cow is *babysit!*"

Young bull: "You dribble regurgitated grass!"

Old bull: "You're so full of…bull droppings!"

I must say, though, that listening to those magnificent-sounding bulls was an unforgettable letdown. When people hear two testosterone-soaked males lobbing threats, insults, and name-calling at each other, bugle-listeners expect to hear a fight. As much bugling as we listened to, we never even heard the air crack from a single horn-clashing. Furthermore, I was convinced that the bull by the house didn't even have any cows to defend. If he did, we didn't hear an elk-chirp out of them. It was nothing more than ballyhoo that I couldn't drown out with earplugs, fans, the radio, sound machines, or cussing.

All kidding aside, listening to elk bugle has always been entertaining, just not as entertaining as listening to them bugle into a vacuum hose with the vacuum on would be.

The kids' best cow Annabelle cleaning off her new calf. The day Annabelle has her calf is always a highlight during calving season. When Annabelle has her calf it's always the topic of discussion at supper that night and our family conversations usually lead to praising Annabelle's motherly attributes. (*Photo by Amy Kirk*)

Calving

When the first calf arrives and is alive and well, we're encouraged and hopeful about the season ahead. We quickly develop a calving routine of cow-checking, feeding, monitoring, sorting, worrying, assisting, turning out, getting a calf to suck, getting cows in, and watching, give or take, repeated daily. After the first big wave of calves is born, things gradually change.

It doesn't take long for sleep to take priority over personal hygiene. When checking at 12, 2, and 4 (or 1, 3, and 5 a.m., take your pick) we handle complications that can easily turn a half hour check into a two-hour ordeal before getting back to sleep. I bother less with good hygiene habits like showering, changing my work clothes, combing my hair, and eating wholesome foods, if I have the option to sleep. As added stress and worry grind on over every cow-calf pair, spousal quibbling can sometimes replace spousal pleasantries.

I delight in seeing new baby calves running pell-mell around the calving pasture at feeding time. Their presence is a real bright spot amidst the relentlessness of calving responsibilities and makes all the challenges, hardships, and sleeplessness worth it.

Spring calving season is a lot of hard work physically and mentally. We live in an area where late Spring snowstorms and freezing cold temperatures are commonplace; making calving a challenge no matter when ranchers set their calving dates. Worrying about and ensuring the survival of new calves and the health of the mothers who bear them is energy-draining.

Calving season is the ranch equivalent to the NCAA's "March Madness." It's an intense time when anything can happen and when most of our family's famous ranch stories are born. The prerequisites of a good calving season story are when our guard is down, we lack sleep, suffer freezing cold temperatures, Spring snowstorms, temperamental cows, or when several cows decide to calve at once, making for short tempers, and numerous problems to sort out simultaneously in the morning.

Calving is a prime time when ranch couples really get to know each other. It promises plenty of uninterrupted couple time—checking cows, getting a cow in, and helping a calf get off to a good start. Art and I make up for all of the date nights we didn't have by checking cows and monitoring calves and feeding the herd together. Calving season is also the most likely time when spouses feel uninhibited to be themselves. They bicker, yell when frustrated, sometimes throw tantrums, and get snippy with each other—compliments of stress and sleep deprivation.

Calving season is a bittersweet time of year. Art and I start out excited, optimistic, well-rested, and patient with each other. By the time the last cow calves, we're glad the season is over because by then the whole herd is sick of us coddling them and we're tired of them.

Making Calving Season Attractive

A ranch wife doesn't have to feel neglected during calving when other females (aka cows) are getting all of her husband's attention. Regaining attractiveness to a husband just takes initiative and creativity.

I'm already involved in my husband's work, so I might as well make the job of calving more enjoyable for all involved and still get some attention. I do this in a number of ways. Whenever I'm not tending to kids, housework, or a cook pot, I surprise my husband by getting all dolled-up. I put on my grubby coveralls, raggedy chore coat, and muddy overshoes. Early mornings I whisper in his ear so we don't wake up the kids and we go check cows together. I can be quite fetching to him when I bring coffee for us and offer to hold the spotlight or ear-tagger for him. Getting the gate eagerly instead of with dread, always raises his eyebrows at me too. I don't exactly skip over to open the gate, but I don't comment that getting gates is the only reason he married me either.

Instead of adding to his aggravation throughout calving, I try to deduct it. My biggest deduction is minimizing how much I talk. I limit how many questions I ask about the day's plan, how many times I ask the same question and try listening without interrupting. He loves it when I'm quiet and observant, allowing him to do the talking instead. Occasionally, our eyes lock-on and I seduce him with my flattering lips—lips that compliment his cow knowledge and tell him how impressed I am. He finds me even more charming when I volunteer to check cows for him.

I leave him bewildered when I don't try to deviate, distract, or suggest a different way of doing his cow-checking and chores routine as I normally do. I also show how much I desire to be involved with him by keeping a calf record book of my own instead of borrowing his. I bring it along with a pen while we're out checking in case he forgets his and needs to record new calves.

When he comes into the kitchen for breakfast or dinner, his jaw drops when he sees me setting his favorite foods on the table that I rarely make: hamburger and beans and cream corn out of a can. I can draw him in like a magnet just by holding a plate of his favorite dessert too, yellow cake with chocolate frosting. I'm very stunning when I keep comments to myself about the junk food he eats if he needs a quick snack that he can eat on the fly.

I like being a big tease and incorporate humor after helping get a difficult cow in, ear tagging a calf with a feisty mother, or after doctoring, if my husband acts testy. Wit is very becoming in ranch women. Sharing ranch-related jokes or stories are great pick-up lines after stressful calving moments. I can always get him to smile at me when I reference our favorite inside jokes or movie lines if he appears stressed and humor is appropriate for particular situations.

Calving season can be attractive for any ranch wife. You just have to slip into something more comfortable and visit your husband at work.

Similarities with Calving Time

The first few weeks of calving season are similar to having a baby for the obvious reason: it's painful to go through, but there are other similarities between calving time and being a new mother:

- Time helps in forgetting how painful either are, enabling the experience to happen all over again.
- Both of our kids, like many of our cows, decided it was time to go into labor prior to a snowstorm.
- Before my babies were born, I prepared and stocked up on infant care supplies, toilet paper, milk, and Advil, so I wouldn't have to go to the store for a while. With the exception of infant supplies, the same list applies prior to calving season. In addition to my husband gathering up calving equipment and supplies he stocks up on his own necessities: Bud Light and Copenhagen.
- The difference between the due date and the actual arrival date of each of my babies was my main focus. Likewise, every year's calving start date and actual

arrival of calves is my husband's and my main focus.

- The excited anticipation of having my baby or calving time starting, is short lived. At the onset of calving season starting or delivering a baby, the anticipation changes to wishing it was all over.
- Once the pains of feeling the labor start, it didn't fail to get progressively worse, more intense, and make me feel out of control of the situation. The work involved during calving season has the same effect.
- Whether calving time or having a baby, both require me to maintain a level of constantly pushing hard when exhausted.
- Babies and calving season steal my sleep, consume most of my time, and sap all of my energy the first few weeks of either of their arrival.
- Babies and calving time force me into keeping odd hours in order to monitor and take care of the baby's needs or check heifers and help my husband with high maintenance new calves or cows needing extra attention.
- Handling a newborn or calving season duties has given my husband and me at times a special feeling: being overwhelmed.
- In the beginning of the change in routine due to the arrival of an infant or a slew of baby calves, I lose things—with the exception of weight—namely sleep, patience, my coffee cup, the reason I went into a room, thoughts, what I was saying, and items I'd just had in my hand.
- Problems beyond the new disruption in my life never fail to plague me at the same time or command equal attention simultaneously.
- Intended to be temporary, abnormal behavior oftentimes morphs into habitual behavior: making my family eat leftovers for supper five out of seven meals and allowing myself to look like a homely mess.
- The first few weeks also typically require getting accustomed to convincing my brain that cat naps are the equivalent of a good night's rest.
- I go through a mess of long nights before it gets better.
- When calving season or the baby finally arrives, relief is only temporary. Other concerns soon follow like worrying if I'll ever have time to catch a nap.
- Some days feel like an eternity will pass before the intense busyness slows down, but I have no choice but to push on through because there's no turning back.
- Once things do slow down, new problems generally replace them.

Like past labor and deliveries, when I look back on the pain of calving season, I realize it was short-lived and I forget all that I went through. About the time the stressful calving season finally wanes, my husband says, "Around the 15ᵗʰ of May we'll turn out the bulls."

The OB Ward and Nursing Home Ranch

The problem with deferring replacement heifers too long is that come calving time, you're apt to end up with a lot of old cows and a bunch of young, first-time calvers to take care of simultaneously.

Hanging on to cows too long and not incorporating younger cows into the herd steadily, creates more calving work than necessary, or so we've found. For a few years we dropped our cow numbers due to drought conditions. We continued to cull cows and weren't able to justify keeping replacement heifers with a shortage of hay and grassy pastures. We always had good intentions on keeping our heifer calves in order to gradually replace some of the older cows, but we ended up selling the replacement heifers as a result of a shortage of grass and a hay crop and a lack of funds to buy hay for additional cows.

Eventually we were able to swing keeping some heifers, but by the time they were ready to calve as two year olds, some of our gentlest, best mother cows in the herd were showing signs of having maxed out their calving health vitality and mothering abilities.

Mid-calving season one year, we had one old cow after the other needing doctoring, helping, or watching. Difficulty in getting up, injuries caused from slipping on icy terrain, lameness, and lack of milk or gumption to attend to a calf were all issues we had to deal with in the older cows.

We made it easier to care for those gals by putting them in a lot with corrals, where they were close to water and feed. The corrals became somewhat of an assisted living area for less-mobile cows.

Then we had our heifers. Young cows are notorious for being difficult to sort off from the rest of the herd and can get squirrely when handled, so we kept them nearby also for easier handling. That was useful when we wanted to put some heifers in the barn or we needed to run them through the head-catch to help them.

Most of our heifers calved alright on their own, but we had to help some of these first-time mother cows deliver their calves. If their calves were big or backwards, we intervened using the head catch to contain the cow and used a calf puller to pull out the calf and save both cow and calf. Heifers that were a bit confused or baffled by their own offspring, which is not unusual, we would use the head catch to keep the cows standing still and point their calves in the right direction to find their mother's milk.

If a cow that was starting to calve tried to claim another cow's calf we had to straighten out the mix-up in the maternity ward (aka barn). Some pairs needed extra time to bond in the barn before being ready to be turned out which involved bringing the cow feed and water until the pair seemed mothered up good.

Nursing chilled calves, doctoring cows that didn't clean right away, monitoring heifers starting to calve that hold off once put in the barn, getting calves to suck, and straightening out the problems in the barn has given me a whole new level of admiration for doctors, nurses, and aides. I admire them for getting to work with human patients.

Dreaming of Sleep

Of all of the dreams I want to come true, my biggest dream is of getting sleep during calving season. When freezing temperatures show up, my husband and I start cow checking at night more consistently.

Night checks can take up to three hours if there are problems, leaving my husband and me sleep deprived even more than normal during calving season. Sleep deprivation makes me wake up feeling dopey; hang-overish from a short night, and craving more of that short-lived pleasure called sleep.

Lack of zzz's makes people do things they wouldn't normally do under well-rested circumstances, like drink decaf coffee. Exhaustion messes with you, not to mention makes a mess of you. I'll shower less in order to sleep more. A hot shower becomes the highlight of the week. Fortunately, I've discovered a body fragrance that masks my body odor really well when I haven't showered enough. It's a Springy-scent that evokes memories of a newborn calf with a hint of cow colostrum and notes of green muck. It's a totally organic fragrance that I won't soon forget and that masks my body odor quit well.

"I always know I slept good when I have drool on my face."

~Reneé age 10

With each additional night that I'm shorted on rest, my motor skills deteriorate. One night it took me a few minutes and some rancher-choice words to realize that the reason I couldn't get the gate to open was because I was opening it at the wrong end. Sometimes it takes me twice as long to check at night because I can't remember the ear tag numbers of cows that I saw that had calved or which cows I just spotlighted.

Sleep deprivation also makes me lazy. I'll deliberately fix soup or crockpot suppers until my family protests. To avoid having to pre-treat and wash four tons of heavily soiled laundry, I'm OK with wearing the same sweatshirt and jeans for several days.

"My eyes aren't really working." (not awake yet)

~Reneé age 8

I progressively cut more corners to improve my night-checking PR (personal record) time when I get rummy-headed. I'll start out piling my jeans and sweatshirt next to the bed so I can put them on in the dark, in my sleep. By mid-calving season, I leave my overshoes in my coveralls by the door and just pull my coveralls over my sleepwear like a fireman to save seven seconds.

It's not beneath me to use bribery, either. Promising myself an afternoon nap temporarily stops my head from whining about being tired. Playing head games with myself keeps me motivated during daylight hours until the daily chores and work gets done, but my mind has a mind of its own when I'm overly tired and try to force sleep.

As a light fall-asleeper, if I'm not plagued with reminders, to-dos, and don't-forgets, then it's the sound of the heater kicking on, my husband's snoring, or being bounced out to the edge of the bed in the wake of his shifting and rolling over in his sleep. When do I finally start to doze off, all I see is a continuous reel of cows lumbering into the barn, muck everywhere, and water balloon-like birth sacs or feet protruding out of cows' backsides.

> *"Mommy, they won't stay open." (eyes)*
> *~Reneé age 3*

To comprehend why I voluntarily give up sleep for cows, I'll have to get back to you on that. I need to sleep on it first.

Noisy Eating Habits Are a Good Sign

The sound of loud slurping and smacking noises indicates that life is being sucked into a calf. Hearing those unmannerly noises are also what restore harmony between my husband and me while we work together to get a calf to suck.

The contentedness between Art and me is sometimes contingent on whether a new calf has gotten up and sucked yet, and hearing the calf eating noisily is a sure sign that the calf has. One of the recurring squabbles between Art and me has been over whether a calf got its mother's milk in its belly.

> *Amy: "Myles, I thought you'd eat better than that."*
> *Myles: "I'm just like the bulls; I waste it."*
> *~Myles age 8*

The teamwork attitude that he and I preach to our kids sometimes gets kicked out of the barn when a new calf hasn't sucked for its first time and we're short on sleep, patience, and love. Our number one rule once a cow's licked her calf off is for the little bugger to get its mother's warm milk into its belly *pronto*. On a cold night, time is crucial with calves that don't appear to have sucked yet. When it's freezing out, we can't give calves a lot of time to figure it out on their own and will intervene in order to keep a calf alive. It's in the middle of the night when my husband and I usually have only half of our wits about us that turns us into two short-tempered halfwits working together to save a calf's life.

The air in the barn can get filled with tension, frustration, pressure, and stress until we're sure a new calf has gotten its belly full of milk. To help ease the pressure when getting a calf to suck doesn't go smoothly, Art and I will sometimes go through a process of elimination in order to keep the calf alive. The most popular steps taken include (in no particular order): critiquing, criticizing, blaming, shouting, taking over the other's job, or a combination of all five.

When time is critical, tension builds with little gripes over our reactions to every problem. Such problems include getting the pair in the barn, opening and closing gates, reading the cow's number, checking the cow's teats to see if they look sucked, checking the calf's condition, arguing whether the cow should be milked into a bottle first and fed to the calf, critiquing milking techniques, or disputing whether the calf got enough milk before turning the pair out of the barn.

When we're feeling rummy-headed tired and trying to get a calf to suck on its own at four in the morning, there's nothing we'd rather hear more than the sound of a noisy eater. The sooner we hear smacking and slurping the sooner we can go back to bed. Getting the little bugger to figure out how to feed itself makes us instantly relieved. A calf that slurps and smacks while eating is a sign of a happy ranch couple.

Once we've overcome the difficulties of getting milk into a calf's belly, the next best sound in the world is when I wake myself up because I'm snoring so loudly.

Labor Pains

Sometimes the labor involved to help a cow that's in trouble is nothing but a big pain. I can relate to the motherly instincts cows have, just not their desire to calve alone and unassisted if a cow's a first-timer and having complications during calving or the calf is in jeopardy, the cow's unwillingness to cooperate makes it difficult to assist her. Animals aren't as appreciative of outside help no matter how troubling their situation. Cows can make it a challenge to monitor them for problems.

Art and I may have had our first child during calving season, but I didn't need to be checked on because I abruptly checked in with him when my water broke. At the hospital, I willingly went into a labor and delivery room, anxious to get comfortable. Not knowing what to expect, I was surprised that we were left alone most of the time. I felt insecure about Art and me getting the counting and breathing down and hyperventilating a result of doing it wrong. I welcomed the nurse who assisted us. As labor progressed, I increasingly felt out of sorts. Unlike a cow, I uncharacteristically encouraged others' efforts to ease my labor pain by cooperating fully and sidelined my independent nature and pride.

Cows that are close to calving get taken to the barn if weather conditions are too risky for calving in the elements. Some cows try to run off or dodge being steered away from their secluded spots. I think my husband would've enjoyed it had I run off when the snowstorm hit while I was in labor. As it was, I would hardly let him leave my bedside. He only got to admire my labor room's comfy-looking recliner from my bedside, and he had to ask my permission for bathroom breaks so that I would release my death grip on his hand. I hesitated but agreed only if he hurried. I didn't let go of him until the contraction subsided, and he was expected back before the next one started. When he didn't make it back before a contraction mounted once, I could only muster one word during the contraction: "**HAND!** (a few short breaths)…**HAND!**" in a hysterical, panic-stricken voice as though I was having a baby or something.

Some women in labor get mad and lash out at their husbands for the painful predicament they're in. Those types make me think of #68. When she calved, she got mean and aggressive protecting her calf when we tried to help her. I wasn't mean, just possessive about being the first to hold and kiss my baby, but I was also lenient in letting nurses tend to my newborn until feeding time. I had no problem letting them take over so I could stockpile sleep before going home to deplete it all. Post delivery I relished eating meals in bed each day and having my own nurse. When it was time to get released, I wanted to bring the hospital staff home with me and that call button thingy to use whenever I needed something.

To help alleviate cow-calf mix-ups, which happen sometimes, we ear-tag calves with ear tag numbers that match their mothers to eliminate confusion if a cow tries to claim the wrong calf. Similarly, hospitals use matching wristbands but they didn't need to worry about me getting confused and claiming a different baby because mine were always the cutest ones there.

The roof-mount spotlight on our little ranch pickup gets used mostly for night checking during calving. (*Photo by Amy Kirk*)

The Bright Side of Calving Season

In order for me to shed some light on calving, I need a spotlight. The difference a spotlight can make is like night and day, but not just any spotlight, one that works.

These gadgets have made finding calving activity at night a lot easier, unless I'm using a light that doesn't work. My husband prefers the kind of spotlight that is permanently mounted on top of his small ranch pickup's roof and is operated from the inside. As a founding member of the "Pringle Poacher Association," (relax, it's just Pringle's local humor) he is very knowledgeable about different spotlights. He knows from experience that roof mount spotlights don't melt vinyl seats, holding onto roof-mount spotlights from inside the cab keep hands warmer than from a four-wheeler and are easier to operate one handed.

> *"We gotta peel our eyes open for cows."*
> – Reneé age 5

The roof-mount types tend to be temperamental about working whenever I use them though. It could have something to do with the spotlights being Pringle modified, wherein the plug-ins get cut off and wires are attached to the dome light connector thingies with black electrical tape instead of being installed according to the spotlight's instructions that we don't have. Usually the problem has more to do with me touching them.

Another popular Pringle modification, for handheld spotlights used in vehicles without cigarette lighters, is cutting off the plug-in and attaching the wires to the vehicle's battery and running the cord through the side window. This is why spotlights are never thrown away. Non-working ones can always be "parted out." True Pringlites own several spotlights and know how to part them out for modification to accommodate different power sources.

As I was saying, it's amazing what I can see at night when I flip the switch on a spotlight that works. I've found that the rechargeable spotlight I use in my jeep really shines in the calving pasture and is especially beneficial to the whole purpose of getting up in the first place, IF the spotlight's been charged up.

Since spotlighting is useful in checking for new calves or calving problems during the night, the most important thing to be looking for, as you might expect, are the ear tag numbers of the cows. When read in the dark, spotlights greatly improve the accuracy of reading the numbers on a cow's ear tag. If a cow or a new calf needs to be checked on later, it's really handy if I know which cow it is. Otherwise they'll always make a liar out of me by being difficult to find again later when I go to show Art.

When I spotlight the herd at night I also use binoculars. I need both the light and the binoculars because sometimes I have to clarify if what I'm seeing is a smallish, balled-up calf or a supersized frozen cowpie. Having such hallucinations when I am sleep deprived have panicked me enough that I couldn't go back to sleep.

As I've found out, it's a good idea to be somewhat alert if not awake when night checking with a spotlight. Being aware of what I'm doing has proven helpful in carrying out the reason for getting up at 2, 3, or 4 a.m. At least once a calving season I will get out to the calving pasture, spotlight a cow with a new calf, reach for the binoculars to get her ear tag number, and realize that I forgot to bring the binoculars.

It was more than a little aggravating the night I went to check at 2 a.m. and every spotlight I tried wouldn't work. The first two attempts I got to the calving pasture before checking to make sure the roof-mounted spotlight worked and the third try I resorted to the rechargeable spotlight, which hadn't been charged.

As long as I remember to make sure the spotlight works before getting out to the calving pasture, spotlights really shine on night checking.

A cow we had been monitoring while calving, all mothered up with her new calf.
(*Photo by Amy Kirk*)

Mothering Up

The intense bond between a mother and her baby is hard to describe to a man in a way that he can really comprehend. The only comparison that would even come close would likely be the bond he feels with his remote.

Since men don't have traveling lunch counters on their chests the way mothers do, guys don't get to experience bonding with their offspring to the degree that a mother does while nursing. Nor do men get to experience the extreme sense of relief that nursing gives when it is way past a newborn's feeding time. Mother's milk is nature's quintessential bonding element.

> *"I'm in the mood for love and snuggle time."*
>
> *~Reneé age 5*

As a mother, I can sympathize with cows that get riled when their bonding time gets interrupted because I've been there. Having to intervene to get a cow's milk in her calf's belly is critical in getting the calf's core body temperature raised to ensure its survival and is the reason ranchers have to interrupt bonding. Ranchers are the EMT's of cattle when a new calf is born in cold temperatures and the calf is still wet and won't suck.

As a first-time mom, all I wanted to do once I delivered my firstborn after nine long months was hold and feed my newborn son, but instead he was whisked away for monitoring. Similar to a chilled new calf taken from a cow in order to warm her baby up and essentially save its life, nurses snatched my son away to NICU (Neonatal Intensive Care Unit) because my baby boy wasn't breathing well. He was monitored closely until he was out of the danger zone the same way a chilled calf is kept warm until it perks up. I waited six hours before I finally got to bond with my baby, nurse him, and sniff his head—I never felt the urge to lick him though. Getting to hold my child before anyone else did was my biggest anxiety. Once I got to hold him, I was willing to share him a little, and from then on I constantly wanted contact with my offspring the way cows do, but especially after visitors who wanted to hold my baby finally returned him to me.

Most cows are wary after calving and won't settle down unless they're left alone to mother-up good. I get that because during my hospital stay I wanted to nurse my newborn alone. Hospital staff and visitor interruptions were distracting and interfered with my mother-child bonding time.

With both of my babies, it was hard to watch my newborn fuss or cry at the hands of another mother and I would get agitated. Emotionally, I was what a rancher would call "breachy," which is a protective and defensive way a cow behaves when she's concerned and anxious to mother-up alone. I especially did not like getting my baby back with foreign smells on him or her that weren't mine and that I didn't like. I would get as restless as a cow eyeing a rancher working on her calf; only baby calves usually respond positively toward ranchers who get them warmed up. At my firstborn's baby shower he did not like other people tending to him. I tried to act unaffected but my baby's cries riled me the way a mother cow will get riled, and I couldn't rip through the baby gifts fast enough in order to get him back.

As a mom, I can attest to the fact that there is no other bond in nature that compares to mothers and their babies. Dads just aren't physically equipped to feed them.

A cute little baldy calf from 2008 calf crop. My favorite springtime routine is getting to see the curious baby calves run and buck around while feeding cows.
(Photo by Amy Kirk)

Baby Fix

I don't miss the days of changing truckloads of dirty diapers, feeling half comatose all the time, and waking up smelling like a dairy barn every morning, but I do occasionally get baby pangs. Spring calving is my oddball way of getting my baby fix.

I enjoyed the newborn stage when our kids were tiny and completely dependant on me to care for them. I could hold and kiss them all I wanted, and there wasn't anything they could do about it. They couldn't get away from me or refuse my obsessive affections. As infants, they slept a lot instead of getting into things I had to worry about, and I didn't have to check on them near as frequently. They never complained about their meals and they were always content just to get fed.

"It was kind of like calf scours; except it wasn't white." (contents of a baby's dirty diaper)
~Myles age 10

I feel similarly about brand-new baby calves. I like taking care of them when intervening is necessary. They give me many opportunities to pet them and they can't run off or kick very hard when they're new. Like human babies, calves develop inquisitiveness toward their environment. They get totally absorbed in watching me the way my kids did during the infant stages of their development.

Back when they drooled more, my kids were smitten with me. They would listen to my voice with interest, and hang onto every word. They'd concentrate on the movement of my lips whenever I spoke to them and watched where I walked, unlike now. It's amazing how drastically their interest in me has changed. Nothing I do or say now gets them so excited that they kick their socks off, and they don't cry for my attention the way they did before they learned to walk and talk and they don't hold their arms up to me for my affections.

When I show up to feed cows and cut the bale twine, baby calves approach me with intense curiosity and watch my every movement. Their facial expressions look as though they're asking, "Whatcha doin'?" Their interest sometimes makes me laugh out loud. Baby calves bunch up behind me, get as close as they dare, and sniff the air between us in an attempt to satisfy their curiosity, then dart off when I turn around.

A lot of my early motherhood days were spent admiring my kids' little mouths, fingers, feet, button noses, and soft fuzzy hair. Since my time isn't absorbed with infant care anymore, I've switched to watching baby calves when I go out to check or feed cows instead. I'm easily amused by calves' little ears perking up when I go by, seeing their tails twitch excitedly as they suckle or touch noses with their mothers and other calves. Watching them buck, hop, or run around like kids on a playground playing tag is highly entertaining.

I tend to linger while feeding cows, just so I can listen to the calves' little noises and watch them play or sprawl out in the sun for a nap like a groggy baby after getting a belly full of milk. I also find it comical to see calves snuggle down into fresh hay near their grazing mothers and munch on the hay surrounding them.

I look forward to regular outings to find out which cows have new calves and to see what their babies look like. When I don't get around calves enough to satisfy my baby fix, I get just as antsy as a hungry baby with a dirty diaper.

Spring Cleanin'

If you have wasted any time reading this book when you could have watched mind-dumbing prime-time television programs, you've probably already concluded that our outfit is a little odd. Now you can confirm it by learning what we consider Spring cleaning.

Late February until late May on the Kirk ranch is the only time of year we see and deal with a common sign that Spring has definitely arrived here: cow cleaning. At our place cleaning is not an activity we engage in, but rather a gloppy, gristly-like substance that pertains to mother cows in Springtime. Cow cleaning refers to the messy piles we get used to looking at and walking around for several months. Wearing rubber dish-washing gloves to handle the cleaning is optional.

Cow cleaning is a ranch term for the placenta that hangs from the back end of a cow and that eventually drops onto the ground after she's calved. At first, cow cleaning is slick and shiny but after it has dropped and been exposed to the ground, barn cats, or our dog, the cleaning loses its sheen. Cow cleaning's sticky surface picks up dirt better than my vacuum.

Cleaning will drop off from a cow anytime from shortly after the cow has calved up to a few days later and is a sign of a healthy cow. If it doesn't fall after a few days, the cow gets prompt and appropriate veterinary treatment to expedite the process. As unattractive as cleaning looks on a cow, it's never something to go tugging on to remove because doing so can do harm to the cow.

To describe cow cleaning to someone who's never seen it, don't ask my husband. He would tell you that fresh cow cleaning resembles one of my favorite pizza toppings—unsliced pepperoni. I would say it resembles a slimy dishtowel and is a naturally recyclable substance.

Dogs are particularly fond of bringing these Mother Nature chew toys to the yard to work on and the only logical place for a dog to eat placenta is in the front yard; preferably near a picture window when guests are looking out the window. These truly organic dog snacks do not come apart easily and will keep our dog entertained for hours. We've witnessed Pepper tugging and gnawing on cow cleaning until she got so worn out she has to take a nap before resuming her snack attacking. Canines will still find old dehydrated placenta tasty midsummer once the cleaning's dried up like a stiff, crispy jerky-flavored rag.

Pepper and the barn cats would likely describe fresh cow cleaning as very chewy. Its texture requires animals to tilt their heads in order to get a good grip on a bite. Cow placentas are nature's long-lasting animal treats. We've never bought dog treats because Pepper finds cow cleaning year-round to chew on. And we're advocates of reusing old stuff. Most cows instinctively eat their own cleaning after they've calved, which is what ranchers prefer to see instead because it provides good nutrients for the cow.

During calving season, I have a hard time getting motivated to do anything that pertains to the activity of cleaning, but taking the time to pick up neglected wads of cow cleaning around the yard does spruce up the place, which is a great idea if we're expecting company. I don't bother with Spring cleaning much unless I can get it to stay on the pitchfork.

Art doing the branding at our neighbor's branding, the Zeimet's.
(*Photo by Amy Kirk*)

Branding

It may not be printed as a national holiday on the rest of the nation's calendars, but branding day is one of the biggest days on our ranch that we recognize every spring.

Really big outfits have more than one branding day, but since we're just a mom and pop operation our branding gets done in a day with the help of good neighbors.

In our young family years, our son was more excited the night before our branding than he was about Christmas. He would sleep in his branding day clothes so he was ready when my husband got him up early to ride and gather our herd. His youthful enthusiasm was a welcome attitude amongst all the stress, anxieties, and worries my husband and I felt preparing for and taking care of prior to our branding day.

Our son's excitement was a good distraction and reminder for us to acknowledge the importance of our family's ranching tradition. The fact that it is becoming a rarity to our area makes it that much more special and unique to our family as an American tradition. Other than no longer sleeping in his clothes, not much has changed for our son since those days. He still looks forward to branding season and calls the spring time of neighboring brandings the "branding circuit."

Our family is lucky to get to carry on this tradition every year. Having a big gathering of friends and neighbors show up to help us get the springtime job done and then put on a big feed for them afterwards as our appreciation is becoming a thing of the past in most parts of the U.S.

And branding day is still just as big of an event in the kitchen, if not bigger, as it is up at the corrals.

Rekindling Branding Day Romance

The romance between my husband and me began in springtime. We'd only been dating a couple of months by branding season and he introduced me to his family on their branding day.

We spent that day, and the rest of those May weekends, helping neighbors gather cows to corrals on horseback, and wrestling calves together to be branded. Our courtship basically evolved throughout those neighborhood brandings, and every May I feel a sentimental twinge about our beginning.

We'd make googley eyes at each other through the thick branding smoke while men hunched over us with vaccine guns. My face would flush pink and I'd start to sweat as the space between us heated up every time those hot branding irons came between us. I felt giddy when he'd wink at me while we bore down to hold a feisty calf as the branding irons marked the calf's hide.

While we wrestled calves, sometimes he'd gaze at me with those hazel eyes and ask, "ANY SCOURS?" while I held down the back end of a calf. After spending all day together at a branding, I could still smell him long after we parted; it was the scent of burnt hair. I spent so much time watching him that I'd forget to pay attention to what I was doing. He'd grab my hand and pull me toward him every time I was about to accidentally sit in fresh manure to hold down a calf.

We'd hold each other's hands while waiting for more calves to wrestle, maybe eat a few Rocky Mountain Oysters off the branding stove, and swig beer from a shared can. Sometimes we'd sneak a quick kiss before grabbing another calf to wrestle for branding, vaccinating and castration (where applicable).

Our branding roles have since changed in the 19 years we've been together. I became busy taking care of our cow kids and preparing the branding day dinners, and he became responsible for making sure all the branding supplies were ready, and lining out the branding crew with the day's work.

For years, I've sorely missed being around my husband on branding day. One year after our kids had reached elementary age, I aimed to rekindle our former branding day romance. I knew it wouldn't be easy to cook dinner and help brand, but I told my husband to get a horse in for me because I intended to be out there.

To be able to do both meant getting up early and staying up late to do as much as possible in advance. The thought of sharing a morning panoramic view of the back ends of cows while riding alongside my husband excited me.

By Sunday morning, I forgot about feeling exhausted, having sore feet, an aching back, and a tension headache. Our daughter and I rode double and I got to admire my husband cowboying, lining someone else out besides me, and our son's horsemanship, as we all gathered cows toward the corrals. My husband ran the branding irons, but we shared a memorable branding day moment when we wrestled one of the kids' calves together so our son could brand it. I spent the day wrestling calves with my son and was only in the kitchen long enough to get the rolls and coffee in the morning, and later, serve and clean up our branding day dinner.

Spending our branding day with my husband *and* my kids turned out to be more romantic than I expected. The extra work was worth the effort but I definitely didn't eat my lunch for free.

How to Feed a Branding Crew

Feeding a branding crew is easy. You just have to know what to feed them. The Holy Grail of a branding day dinner is man food—the kind with substance to it and nothing more. No foofy stuff, unidentifiable herbs, or unusual ingredients.

For starters, when I plan a branding day dinner I don't get ordinary paper plates or go by the recommended serving size amounts for food. Suggested serving sizes are perfect for children but not for a branding crew. Guys who come to our branding fill every space on their plates then stack more layers on top. They like substantial amounts of food after branding which standard paper plates aren't designed for but do make perfect plates for desserts.

"But can you cook in your underwear though?"

- Reneé age 4

When I first took over the branding day dinner duties several years ago, I thought I had to prove myself as a cook and demonstrate my culinary skills against the other ranch wives' cooking. I aimed to impress everyone with different side dishes and exquisite desserts in hopes of dismissing any doubts people might have had about my capabilities to cook and feed a large crew.

Luckily, I'm a fast learner. It only took slightly less than a ton of leftovers to figure out that sticking with good old American cowboy classics eliminated a lot of extra food and, more importantly, work in the kitchen. In addition to roast beef and barbeque ribs, cream corn, beans, mashed potatoes and gravy, coleslaw, pies, basic chocolate cake and brownies were bigger hits than the artisan-type desserts and sides I tried to impress with. The less time I spent making fancy side salads and desserts and replacing them with traditional favorites, the more popular the food became.

For my first branding dinner, I made coffee cake and two kinds of cinnamon rolls to kick off the morning after sorting the cows off the calves was done. I made plain cinnamon rolls for the kids and orange rolls—which I thought were delectable—for the adults. There was nothing left of the plain Jane rolls, and I ate the only piece of coffee cake that was dug out of the pan after eating a roll too. I also had the whole pan of those delectable orange rolls to eat by myself for a week, and once I polished them off I worked on the leftover coffee cake.

"How much mileage will it take to fix supper?"

~Myles age 6

No matter how attractive fruit or vegetable salads are made to look, most cowboys won't eat fruity stuff with their beef, and the only vegetable worth putting out is a lot of mashed potatoes. It's been my observation that the closest food to anything sweet tasting that a branding crew will eat with meat is homemade cream corn. Jell-O doesn't stand up too well at brandings either. The one time I made Jell-O there were only three or four little divots dug out that some kids took. (I think they were mine).

In order to get a branding crew to clean up a salad, it should have some weight to it when put on a plate the way potato salad or dense coleslaw does. Standard meat dishes and classic sides bring out the flavor in a beer, but fruit or vegetable salads tend to kill the flavor of a Budweiser. Fortunately, the ladies who helped me in the kitchen included some of the unpopular dishes on their plate out of pity my first year.

Since I learned to stick with serving man food, cooking for our branding is easy and my new favorite dishes are scraped-clean pots, pans, and bowls.

Art and Myles, neighbor Charlie Zeimet (far right) and friend Jay Miller (far left)
getting ready to help gather the Zeimet family's cattle for their branding day.
(Photo by Roy Miller)

Branding Day Protocol

You may not think a branding requires etiquette but there are certain
expectations that go with attending and/or participating in a branding.

According to an undocumented branding policy, if you want to help
gather cattle, don't be late. Special circumstances can't be helped, but lack of
planning ahead isn't one of them. A rancher goes by his own time on his branding
day, not someone else's.

A branding is not the place to ride a green broke horse or ride a mount
that's never been around cattle before. Riders should bring a horse that knows cows.
The horses don't necessarily have to know the cows personally or know mutual
acquaintances but they do need to have management skills in working with cows.
A horse that blows up, riles other horses, or is difficult to handle can stir up an
otherwise smooth cow-gathering operation.

If a dog owner doesn't want man's best friend to become man's only friend,
bringing a yapping dog or one that chases livestock isn't recommended. A spooked
horse can cause a wreck, and stirred up cows are harder to handle if riled.

Unless you've specifically been asked to, standing in the way of
approaching cattle is a death wish. Nothing irritates a rancher more on his branding
day than having a herd of cattle heading nicely for the corrals and suddenly scatter

because someone's standing in the way. By the time you've been clipped by a rancher's verbal fire power for all to hear, you'll wish you could be stoned to death instead.

If you see a better way to handle cattle, or do a branding chore, by all means do not tell the rancher. Regardless of how senseless or unorganized a rancher's system looks, these are men who have always gathered, sorted and branded a specific way for reasons they probably don't even understand, but don't like people telling them how to run their ranch or branding.

Cattle ranchers typically handpick neighbors they trust to do the important branding jobs and are usually the same people every year. No matter how appealing a job like castrating calves looks, never assume a job unless you're asked to do it. Running a branding iron takes skill and is generally assigned to elder ranchers. Unless they're senile. Old timers know which brand to use, which side and where on the animal to brand, how to place it correctly for identification, and how to avoid smearing or branding too deeply.

Careless or novice vaccine gun operators can waste expensive vaccine if they don't know what they're doing. Most ranchers try to get by as cheaply as possible by buying just enough vaccine for the number of calves they're vaccinating, using only what's recommended, and relying on experienced vaccine gun users to administer it.

Traditionally, a big meal is provided after branding as a token of thanks to those who helped out. If you didn't help out in the branding corral, you're still invited to stay for dinner; just don't be the first in line.

Above all else, the most important thing you should remember to do at a branding no matter where you go is to ALWAYS compliment the cook.

A typical backside of boys' Wrangler jeans on a muddy branding day.
(*Photo by Amy Kirk*)

The Mother of All Branding Day Stains

The mere sight of my teenage son's Wranglers would've killed a normal mom. To most mothers, the mixture of boy, mud, and calf wrestling would've rendered his jeans laundry mission impossible.

Mud may be avoided by moms, clean freaks, Wall Street businessmen, and girls wearing new shoes, but boys have always been there for mud. Through thick or thin, boys don't judge. They accept all kinds of mud. Oh sure, it likes a clean car, but it loves a pair of boy's good, clean Wranglers.

Our boy really wanted to get in on more calf wrestling, so my husband and I agreed to let him go by himself to a couple of brandings close to home. Hefty rain showers prior to the weekend created soggy conditions which made driving on pasture roads to branding locations difficult but fun for boys to wrestle calves in.

By Sunday, my son's Wranglers looked like brown Carhartt jeans. His pants were completely covered in a shell of caked-on mud, thanks to a roper who roped and dragged boys through mud like water skiers for fun after branding was done. Obviously, there weren't any mothers around.

When I saw what my fourteen year old had done to his pants, my first reaction was, "I am not looking forward to laundry day." Getting the mud out of his jeans looked harder than the labor I went through without an epidural to deliver him.

I let his jeans dry completely on the clothes line and decided to blast the chunks off with an air hose, but the dried-on mud was like concrete. It didn't move so I had to painstakingly scrape and chisel the layers off. As I scraped, I came to terms with the fact that the jeans probably wouldn't look the same again, which was aggravating since they were one of three new pairs I'd recently bought to replace the ones he'd outgrown.

I couldn't bring myself to give up on the jeans entirely. Out on the porch, I filled a galvanized tub with water to soak the jeans in a combination of different powders and liquids that have proven themselves as good stain removers on tough laundry impossible missions in the past. In the proper combination, my laundry cleaning super powers could've possibly created an explosion, but luckily nothing blew up when I mixed them in the water.

Once I had the mud scraped off, I didn't bother to do any scrubbing. Scraping was enough work for one day. I worked the jeans into the mixture to stir everything up good and let them soak for two days. Before I transferred them to the washing machine, I agitated and soaked the jeans again, then ran the whole cycle. Fortunately, nothing exploded there either.

Once the cycle was done, I went to see if the jeans had disintegrated from my laundry concoction. If by chance anything was left, I was curious to see how much of the mud stains remained. When I pulled an intact pair of jeans out of the washing machine, I was reminded what a beautiful color denim blue is.

If you must know what my secret laundry super powers were, they included a can of coke, a cup of vinegar, a capful of Murphy's Oil Soap (removes blood stains really well), a handful each of borax and baking soda, and laundry detergent. Bomb suit optional.

This is my favorite picture of the kids' first cow, Annabelle and her 5th calf Tink (Tinkerbell) enjoying the afternoon sunshine. (*Photo by Amy Kirk*)

Memorable Animals

Any time a person works with animals for a living he or she is guaranteed to have a job that is never short of adventures.

Cows especially know how to make life interesting for all involved. At times they can be the Dennis the Menaces of a ranch (multiplied by the number of head of cows a ranch has).

Sometimes their curiosity is what gets them into trouble, causing much strife and anxieties for the people taking care of them. Other times it's their stubborn bovine ways, their not wanting to cooperate when someone just wants to help them. Then there are the cows that cave in to peer pressure assisting a whole bunch of cows to cause a ruckus.

Our cow herd has been the root cause of many a "Monday Morning Special" for me: those ag-related crises that catch a rancher or ranch wife off guard first thing on a Monday morning, but livestock don't limit pulling shenanigans to just Mondays. One of their favorite times of the year to stir up excitement is during calving season when ranch couples are groggy from lack of adequate sleep and not at the top of their game. Calving is the time of year when many cows' dispositions morph. While in the throes of calving, cows' instincts kick in to be protective, defensive, suspicious, defiant, unwilling, uncooperative and moody before, during, and after they've had their calves. These can all make it difficult to help them if their health or their calves' health, well-being, or life is in trouble. It's not easy to reason with a cow when her hormones are jacked up.

Every rancher has a story about getting chased by a cow, many of which occur during calving season. They can be predictable in their reactions or behaviors but cows like to add a twist to a predictable situation just to throw a handler off. Other times they'll do stuff when being handled that's totally unexpected and catches the handler off guard.

If our cows aren't busy making our life interesting getting out through a fence, chasing us up a fence, or getting in someone's yard, then the barn cats' amusing behavior and antics, our dog's ball-fetching obsession, or our horses' patient babysitting ways oblige us.

The Eighth Wonder of the World

Most people aren't aware that South Dakota has two wonders of the world: Mount Rushmore and our Hereford cow Annabelle—the Eighth Wonder of the World.

A neighboring rancher said once that a Hereford cow that doesn't get pinkeye, sunburned udders, and doesn't prolapse, is the Eighth Wonder of the World. Hereford cattle are known for these problems as much as they are for their gentle disposition.

Annabelle is a natural wonder and is regarded with awe for more than one reason. She was an orphaned twin of one of our cows that a neighboring rancher found after we moved our herd to summer range back in 2003 and the twin became our kids' first bucket calf.

For whatever reason, we haven't been overly successful in the past getting bucket calves to turn out to be good mother cows. Annabelle was our exception. Since she had her first calf as a three-year old, she consistently produced good calves and was a good momma. Her heifer calves were kept as replacement heifers to build the kids' herd and bull calves were sold in the fall with our calf crop and the money was put toward Myles and Reneé's college fund.

Annabelle possessed the best mothering qualities that a rancher could ask for in a cow. Every year she calved on her own and always had her calf immediately licked clean and up and sucking shortly after it was born. She was the superstar of our herd and the highlight of every calving season.

The arrival of her calves as well as her daughters' calves were always highly anticipated. Being the first one to see Annabelle's new calf one year made my having to get up at 3:30 in the morning worthwhile. I took great satisfaction in getting to be the first one to know Annabelle had calved and getting to tell the family the good news that morning.

Despite calving when the temperature was in the teens that year, Annabelle had taken care of "Anna Maria"—what the kids named her calf—so well that the calf acted like she was a week old instead of hours old. When my husband came in from his daylight cow check that morning and saw Annabelle's new calf, he said of our only Hereford cow, "She's the best cow on the place!"

Not only had Annabelle turned out to be a good mother and one of the gentlest cows, she was one of the healthiest cows of the whole herd, another marvel considering that many cows would run her off at feeding time. Her heifer calves always matured into gentle mother cows also.

When she was just a bucket calf, we didn't realize how many life lessons Annabelle would end up teaching our kids. Myles and Reneé learned what it meant to be depended upon, and having Annabelle developed their compassion for animals. Through Annabelle, they understood the important role of agriculture, the reality of being a rancher, and what investing in something really means: hard work, patience, time, and energy. Partaking in the ranch work as part of their ownership of cows, our kids now have a much better understanding of reproduction and birth, as well as the harsh realities of death.

As my husband and I once were marveling over the calves from Annabelle's bloodline, he said, "What we're doing for these kids by having Annabelle around is building up a good herd of gentle cows for them"—each one a souvenir from one of the Wonders of the World worth treasuring.

Pepper with one of thousands of tennis balls she's fetched. (*Photo by Reneé Kirk*)

Keep an Eye on the Ball

Blue Heeler dogs are common on ranches because of their desire to have jobs to do. Our dog Pepper is no exception. She loves to fetch.

Pepper is a Blue Heeler-Border Collie tennis ball fetcher. Baseballs and softballs aren't chewy enough and footballs, basketballs, and soccer balls are hard for her to retrieve.

Our dog makes up her own rules for the game of fetch. The most important rule being that no other dogs are allowed to play with her. She lets them know that fetch is a one-dog game around here.

> *"She sure is loyal to that ball."*
>
> *-Myles age 10*

Pepper will use any means necessary to get someone to throw a ball, such as dropping a dirty, slobbery ball on a person's shoes or lap—regardless of her attire—on her lawn chair, or in a basket of clean, line-dried laundry. Pepper knows from past experience that this tactic is extremely effective in getting the person to throw it.

Chewing and slobbering on the ball for at least twenty seconds before dropping it for the thrower is part of the game. It's how she breaks in new tennis balls but it has become a habit with old ones too. Equipment such as the "Chuck-It" is permitted since it ensures more ball-throwing. The Chuck-It is a hand-held, far-flinging, hands-free-from-touching-the-slimy-ball, arm-saving, ball launcher, and is rated number one among ball-throwers, especially with people who aren't fond of picking up slimy balls.

> *"It's like a roundish ball."*
>
> *~Myles age 6*

A tennis ball is game-worthy regardless of its condition. It can be split open, hanging by a piece of felt, and not able to bounce, but as long as it can sail through the air it's allowed.

Pepper will give herself a head start anytime someone's hand moves toward a ball. Fetch can be played any time of day and she will try to get a game going anywhere. Her favorite places are where someone's trying to work, like flowerbeds, flowerpots, the vegetable garden, the shop, or the sandbox, and a game lasts until the ball-thrower gets tired.

If the ball hasn't moved in a long time and Pepper feels a thrower is stalling, she permits herself to pick it up and drop it repeatedly in order to get the thrower's attention or to remind him or her to throw it. If kids deliberately bury it in the sandbox or cover it up with dirt, digging it up is acceptable and anytime the ball gets bumped or rolled out of the way, it counts as a throw.

If ball throwers play dirty and put the ball where she can't reach it, she will sit, wait, and watch the spot where she knows the ball is until someone gets it down or the ball drops. Tennis balls are found in hanging flower baskets, the porch swing, the hole in the center of the outdoor table, wedged between tree branches, and in folding chair cup holders.

Pepper calls her own time outs and will take the ball with her under a vehicle until she's rested but if someone grabs the ball before she's ready, she HAS to fetch it. A thrown ball can never be ignored.

She keeps a ball at the ready 24/7 in case there's a new novice (aka "sucker") to recruit. Once a visitor is deemed harmless to the family, she'll initiate a game. Her favorite recruits are naïve children, politicians, new UPS or Schwan's guys, and people unfamiliar to the game.

Pepper loves tournaments wherein several people are around to play fetch because what's most important to our ranch dog: that she has a ball.

Reneé and Birde hangin' out at the Custer County Fair Play Day Rodeo.
(*Photo by Amy Kirk*)

Birde Lover

When I saw a bumper sticker that said, "Have you hugged your kid today?" I couldn't help but think about our babysitter, Birde, (pronounced like bird) whom I hadn't hugged lately.

After contemplating those I've neglected, I realized our kids' babysitter needs a lot more appreciative squeezes from me. I don't know of any ranch family that hasn't had a good ol' horse at one time or another that's been well-trusted with their kids. Our babysitter horse, Birde, has always eased my mind whenever our kids or their guests wanted to ride. Sometimes I've trusted Birde more than a young adult in taking care of our kids.

> *"Birde is a gentleman."*
> *~ Reneé age 5*

His papered name, "Ezzy Jet Birde," makes one think he might have nabbed a little speed in his pedigree, but in truth, he's so laid back he's borderline lazy, which inspired his nick name, "Birde The Lazy Turd." His calm demeanor matches that of our daughter, which makes the two a perfect fit. Reneé isn't interested in hot horses she can't handle and likes being in control when it's time to take off on a lope.

Of our meager remuda, Birde's the curious one, always coming up to greet us if we're nearby. He likes anybody's company but enjoys even more the companionship of kids around petting, grooming, and feeding him. We trust Birde the most with novices whenever young guests from town who are unaccustomed to being around horses ask the inevitable question, "Can we ride the horses?" Birde doesn't spook when kids holler or dart around him and he endures being saddled and bridled by inexperienced little people wanting to do it themselves.

> *"I'm only invented to sit on right! (giving Reneé horseback ride)"*
>
> *~Myles age 7*

Birde's patience with young riders combined with his docile temperament and understanding of the nature of inattentive kids around, makes him a favorite among kids and adults. Even when our kids were tikes, I had no qualms about putting our youngsters on him. Our kids developed their riding skills and confidence with horses on Birde because he reins easily and tolerates being handled by them. He's not restless but rather stands still while getting saddled no matter how long it takes kids to clamber up by saddle strings, stirrups, or any other means in order to make it onto his back, which to a kid, a horse that stands 15 ½ hands high can seem a long way up.

> *"I'm like a colt: I got big teeth and skinny legs."*
>
> *~Myles age 9*

Since Birde and Reneé aren't eager to chase down a cow with lightning speed, they make a good pair for bringing up the rear when moving cows. Birde doesn't get wound up and take off when other riders leave to wrangle runaways or strays.

Birde takes good care of our kids and has a likeable disposition, but due to his timid nature, he's lost his rank in the pecking order to one of our younger, more aggressive, and appropriately named gelding, Bean Dip, or Bean for short. Even though Birde's the second oldest horse on the place, he gets run off at feeding time, so we make sure he's paid accordingly for his babysitting services.

He may not hold any records for jet-fast speed, but he's a champion for soundness and kid-tested sitter approval for which I love him. Have you hugged your babysitter today?

Pepper and her adored companions. (*Photo by Martha Studt*)

Save Companion Time

My name is Pepper. I'm the Kirk Ranch dog. I am probably barking where no dog has barked before to protest, but it's time that I put my paws down and bark louder. Maybe even growl.

The school where my "kids" attend starts way too early and, quite frankly, I don't like it one bit. I spend all stinkin' winter waiting around for summer to arrive so my companions and I can be together outside.

Summer days may be long (and at times, they can be very pant-worthy), but they're too short on account of school. Oh how I dread seeing that yellow bus. There's no bark to explain it. During the school year I have to wait all day for my pals to get home, and then they usually have sports practices and stuff to do inside until dark. Not cool; even once it gets cold out.

Don't schools know what a school's early start does to outside dogs like me? The summer season's gotten ridiculously shorter and I OBJECT! Spending summer months with my kids is the stuff my dreams are made of and this early-start thing is worse than fleas. During the summer, the kids and I are busy doing stuff outside where I can follow them around, watch them, and go places with them, namely all the spots that I marked last time.

The most satisfying times of my life are having my companions with me to sleep outside. I curl up on their sleeping bags and stay there until they wake up. Unless of course I hear the sound of the front door opening which might mean food that I can't bear to let the barn cats discover. Outdoor sleepovers have been our summer tradition, but school starting early ruins it!

I don't need anything else when my buddies and I are together. Well, except maybe a refreshing sloppy drink of water and an occasional plunge in the nearby dam or stock tank when it's hot. The best sound in the world is hearing my pals holler, "PEP! LOAD UP!" I always know it means we're headed somewhere together that's fun and an adventure for dogs! I love riding along to check salt, water tanks, and cows and smelling the air from the back of a pickup. If I'm lucky, cows are out and I get to chase them back where they belong. When my kids and I are together, I can stay very busy finding rabbits to chase, a mouse trail to sniff, and general snooping around.

When we go to the heifer pasture, I get to run all the way to the stock tank where we pump water to fill it up. No human can know how good it feels to lope through tall grass, feeling it graze my face and ribs then jumping in the stock tank to cool off and lap up a drink of water at the same time.

Helping scatter deer out of the alfalfa field with my boy is so exhilarating that I can hardly contain myself until I'm told to "Go get 'em!" when I see deer out there. It ranks right up there with fetching tennis balls.

As you can see, I strongly disapprove of the school year starting early. When quality companion time gets compromised, it just gets my hackles up.

Cat Tales

Barn cats serve a useful purpose on a ranch: they keep the mice and pack rat population down, but they also entertain us.

Rodents are destructive to equipment and buildings, and barn cats are kept around to hunt them for us. Our barn cats usually don't get named, but the ones we acquired from other ranch families with too many, came with names. If my kids were lucky enough to catch some, they got names as kittens.

"Did you know them cats are slobs?"

– Reneé age 5

Patches was given to us and was a light-colored calico and an excellent hunter yet tame enough to pet. She was a good momma that showed her kittens how to hunt. When we adopted her, my daughter was two and would mimic me calling Patches by saying, "Baaaa-ch-ezzz."

Morrisette was another calico female already named, from a young couple in town who couldn't have pets but fed the stray whenever she showed up on their porch. They said she was really wild, but that they'd tamed her and were willing to deliver her to us. When they brought her down, the poor guy holding the cat should've tried to save his arms instead of saving face about saying she was tame. He tried to set Morrisette down to pet and release her slowly out of the towel she was wrapped up in. Instead, the cat shredded his arms until he let her go, upon which she bolted and wasn't seen again for two weeks before she eventually came back and stayed.

Blackjack was an all-black male that my son decided was his barn cat. The cat impressed my son when it came strutting up to the shop with a small limp snake in its jaws. Pumpkin Jack was a black cat my daughter named because she liked the idea of having a Halloween cat. The kids found and caught Pumpkin Jack as a kitten because he was so weak from being orphaned and starved. Once grown, Pumpkin Jack had legs that stayed short due to his stunted growth before being found; watching him hunting in our field entertained us.

Our favorite barn cat was a blue-gray striped male my daughter named Blueberry. He came from another ranch that we've gotten barn cats from before when they got overrun with kitten litters. Blueberry wasn't intimidated by our dog Pepper and would sleep in the dog house with Pepper instead of outbuildings and they always got along.

During the winter, my family and I chuckled whenever Blueberry was found warming himself in Pepper's empty heated water dish. Unfortunately, Blueberry's curiosity got him locked up a lot. He often got shut in my car by accident while I went back and forth to the house to unload groceries. He got zipped inside the kids' tent by mistake for a day once and another time he couldn't get out of the garden shed because I had shut him inside not realizing that he'd followed me in. Fortunately, he knew how to get our attention and we were always able to see or hear him in time.

Our favorite Blueberry story was his ride on top of a hay bale on the way to feed cows. My husband noticed a shadow casting the silhouette of a cat on top of the round bale loaded on the bale bed pickup as he backed out of the shop to feed cows. It wasn't until the bale was set on the ground that Blueberry jumped off and trotted back to the shop. Blueberry had the most interesting adventures.

Country cats like Blueberry may not be around anymore, but we hang onto our cats by their tales.

A Barrel Horse

Growing up, I dreamed about being a barrel racer someday but should've considered being a saddle bronc rider instead. I got a lot more practice in on that kind of horse event.

The horses of my youth weren't papered (registered) or have fancy pedigrees and were rarely sound animals. They each had at least one well-established character flaw we had to deal with, but everyone in my family had something to ride. One was head-shy and a bugger about getting his back feet shod, one foundered easily, another had a penchant for eluding anybody toting a halter and one had a mountain ridge for a backbone making it impossible to ride him bareback.

"It was like the Pony Express gone wild!" (Riding Poquito, the kids' pony)
~Myles age 11

When I was about eight, my dad bought a couple of horses that were inseparable. One was a buckskin mare named Pretzels who'd only had the dirt ridden off her and the other had a lot to be desired. He was a tough-looking, fat, barrel-bellied, swayback chestnut gelding named Scruffy who lived up to his name.

Pretzels, the buckskin mare, wasn't well broke when we got her, and Scruffy knew only a tad more than she did. Namely tricks. He liked it best when I wasn't on his back and was always trying to figure out ways to get me off my saddle by any means necessary so he could do more enjoyable things like scratching his belly on one of the shrubs in front of the house, which annoyed my mother. He also habitually tried to use me as a rubbing post to get his bridle or halter off.

"He's got a Hemi motor in him." (horse on a movie)
~Myles age 9

Scruffy demonstrated his behavioral skills with fervor. When my dad and I went to help a neighbor and his two boys gather some cows, the oldest boy rode Pretzels, but the neighbor kid made the mistake of getting off to fetch a can of chew that had dropped on the ground. In the process, Pretzels got away from him and bee lined for their barn upon which Scruffy bolted to follow with me on board. I pulled on the reins hard, but it wasn't enough and I got dumped. The last thing I remember before the lights went out was seeing a flat rock in the tall grass and hearing my dad hollering, "PULL ON THE REINS!... PULL ON THE REINS!" When I came to, I was sprawled out on a couch looking up at the neighbors' two daughters talking and hovering over me; and I was fuming that I got left behind.

Scruffy preferred sticking to his old ways when I tried to introduce him to showmanship, which he really didn't care about. He excelled more at fighting my commands and being uncooperative. What I remember about showmanship amounts to the time he started bucking while practicing and my riding him for a couple of jumps before bouncing off the ground. I watched a dust trail billow behind him and my little black stirrups slapping his ribs wildly as he bucked and high-loped it into the setting sun.

He was used to doing things his way before we got him, and at times it was a battle for me to control him or stay in the saddle. He'd try peeling me off on low-hanging tree branches or use friction to serrate my knee on the nearest pine tree or post and at any creek crossing he encountered he would try to leap-frog over it instead of plodding through like normal horses. It generally took wearing him down and sweating the resistance out of him to make riding him less work. In the end, the closest I ever got to riding around barrels was settling for riding a barrel-bellied horse instead.

Paying Tribute to Cows

I am grateful for cows. They provide many things for my family besides tasty, protein-packed beef, and I feel they deserve a little praise.

For starters, my family has cows to thank for our livelihood. Taking care of cows is a steady job, one that's challenging and secure. Even in lean years when the cattle market took a nosedive, regardless of cattle prices our herd has always given us plenty of work to do.

Taking our kids along at an early age to check cows during calving season helped simplify the job of clarifying where babies come from. When my son was six, he delighted in explaining in detail to me as well as all the ladies at his sister's baby shower, how calves were born after watching his dad pull a backwards calf. He and his sister have witnessed many calves being born and have both experienced firsthand the realities of death.

Cows also provide many health benefits. Working for them is a stand-up job. Taking care of them keeps my family active and physically fit by making us walk, climb, and/or sometimes sprint to handle, sort, or load them. We also get strength training through pitching hay, packing five gallon buckets of feed, 50 pound salt blocks, or rolling 250 pound mineral lick tubs out of a stock trailer. Lastly, our cattle give us sustenance: healthy, nourishing, and satiating beef.

Managing cows has been paramount in helping us maintain a humble, modest lifestyle also. Relying on an income that's dependent upon fluctuating livestock prices has encouraged us to live within our means.

Cows have helped us illustrate to our kids what it means to be responsible for something other than themselves and to be committed to a job. Before pursuing our own interests, we always take care of livestock first. Handling livestock responsibilities has also proven to our kids that after doing chores to their parents' expectations, other responsibilities are easy in comparison.

Our kids have observed that owning cows means less money for themselves or essentially no money if they don't rely on their resourcefulness whenever possible. Dealing with problems related to cows has been the best way to teach our kids how to put their ingenuity and skills to work and not be wasteful but to use what's already available to them, which may explain why they are constantly using my stuff. Our cows have made us frugal and industrious. As a result, bad economies have never been devastating adjustments.

Managing a herd of cows is a livelihood that depends on the land and has instilled good stewardship practices like using our resources respectfully. As producers who rely on the land for feeding and raising livestock that will eventually produce our income, we know that taking care of what we have is important. How well we manage the land, water, and livestock determines our livelihood.

Most especially, we help provide a necessary and worthwhile American commodity produced with pride and care; an importance we try to pass on to our kids. Unlike the majority of products made that aren't a necessity of life and especially merchandise made out-of-country that's cheaply made, raising cattle provides vital goods for people in our country and around the globe. With an ever-increasing population, the demand to feed the world is put on the shoulders of people in agriculture.

Raising cows is a lot more work than some people care for, but we don't mind it. In exchange for taking good care of our cows they provide us with everything we need.

In My Next Life I Want To Be a Cow

In my next life I want to be a cow on a United States cattle ranch so I can find out what it feels like to be spoiled. Cows live a cushy life as a result of a rancher's hard work and his pocketbook.

If I were a cow, I would get to eat an abundance of the best feed a rancher could provide and receive it with first-rate service. As a cow, I would never be let down because a rancher is a highly dependable person who would feed me at the same time every day.

These cattle stewards put in most of their time working for their cows—something I can't get my rancher-husband nearly as enthused about doing for me, his wife. I would never have to worry about my welfare on a holiday or over the weekend. As a cow, I would know that under a cattleman's care, feeding and watering livestock takes priority over plans for recreational leisure and vacations. A rancher wouldn't skip a day in feeding me because my care comes first.

No matter what I smelled like or pooped on, a rancher's world would still revolve around me daily. I could poop on him and he'd still plan on us spending the future together if I were one of his cows.

It would be so sweet to know how it feels to be thought about, worried about, fussed over, looked after and checked on like a cow is. I could bleed a rancher's bank account dry with all my needs, and he would just write it off at tax time.

If I were lucky enough to be a cow, I could enjoy being considered a high priority and ranked at the top of a rancher's to-do list every day. Taking care of a cow herd is a rancher's life passion. Ranchers definitely don't do it to get rich because cattle ranching isn't known for its monetary rewards. Being a cow would be an easy way to be ranked #1 for something.

If I wandered off and couldn't get back—which cows are known to do—a rancher would gather me up and get me back home safely. If I was found calving out in a snowstorm, he would get me into a barn, protected from the elements. If I had trouble calving or my new calf wasn't responsive, a rancher would know what to do and act quickly. If I was a cow, I wouldn't need health insurance. I'd get the best of care possible from a rancher. He would notice before I did if my calf or I were sick, and would doctor us up if necessary.

In my next life, if I'm fortunate enough to live a life as a cow on a U.S. cattle ranch, you can call me a cow and I'll consider it an honor. But until then, you can call me Amy Kirk, an agvocate, a columnist, Miss (I'm not too fond of ma'am), Mrs. Kirk, funny, Amy, a writer, witty….

(Photo by Art Kirk)

About the Author

Amy Kirk is a proud born-and-raised South Dakotan and writes a weekly humor column, *A Ranchwife's Slant* when not helping her husband check or feed cows, haul water, or cobble fence. Amy and her husband Art run a Hereford-Angus cow-calf operation near Pringle, South Dakota with the help of their two teenagers, Myles and Reneé. Her column is featured in several Midwestern newspapers and she has also been featured in *South Dakota Magazine*, *Western Horseman*, *Back Home*, and *Ranch & Reata* magazines and the book *Going Somewhere* by Tom Moates.

For more about Amy visit www.amykirk.com, *A Ranchwife's Slant* Facebook page, or her Twitter handle @RanchwifesSlant.

Contact Amy at: amy@amykirk.com
or write her at: Saddlestrings Freelancing, L.L.C.
Amy Kirk
P.O. Box 132
Pringle, SD 57773

CPSIA information can be obtained at www.ICGtesting.com
Printed in the USA
LVOW12s0444210116

471302LV00001B/149/P

9 780984 585069